Alpha Dreamers

Alpha Dreamers

The five billion connected dreamers
who will change the world

Naseem Javed

Metrostate Syndicate

Publisher:
Metrostate Syndicate
Toronto,
www.metrostate.com

Published in United States, Canada

Library of Congress Control Number: 2019931132

Library and Archives Canada Cataloguing in Publication

ISBN: 978-0-9866100-4-2

First Edition - April 2019
Book Design - Corpomundi
Printed and Bound in United States

Soft Cover: USD$ 25.00

www.amazon.com

Publisher Contact:
www.metrostate.com
kw@metrostate.com

For, Lucie, Tashi and Rani

Contents

Contents

PREFACE

A simple philosophy

All based on common sense; create real productivity, produce real value, add honest profitability and serve mankind. Basically, create grassroots prosperity with tolerance and diversity to help surroundings. Save communities to save the planet, create societies of lifelong learners to save harmony. In its raw nature, this thinking already exists as an established mantra and historically practiced in the entrepreneurial realm all over the world. An entrepreneurial mind is a cognizant lifelong learning mind.

If the mind is the miracle of the universe, the body is an amazing temple that houses this gift, mankind has slipped badly on this realization; self-discovery, self-optimization, lifelong learning is where we need to start once again on a new blank page. We must unlearn the fake economies, fake wars and fake solutions. When mankind is in trouble only mankind's rules will solve the issues. The cognizant entrepreneurial mind can handle this.

Today, a billion new entrepreneurs are being added to the world. Historically, some 100,000 entrepreneurs carved out the entrepreneurial supremacy of America that lasted over a century.

A new merging world is opening by the hour. Grassroots prosperity is the number one issue to most of our problems all over the world. Extreme wealth but divided is not the answer, extreme technology but based on destructive entrapments is not the solution. Grassroots mobilization of human talent in harmony and massive deployment of technology to achieve this is now the ultimate challenge. Less dependent on new funding, this philosophy is based on constructive and positive mobilization of currently stranded grassroots entrepreneurialism and global age skills to create local prosperity. Simple.

A quick study of world leaders will put a spot light between the Machiavellian diseased, laced with deceptive shenanigans or the brightly different Entrepreneurial friendly leaderships creating pure raw ethical pursuits of creating grassroots uplifts. The world is awakening to new measurement, with new topics in coming elections around the world. The smarter citizenry is increasingly getting armed with truth and better ideas on how to save their local resources and how to redeploy for local prosperity, save the community, save the nation and save the planet. There is nothing wrong with selective economic nationalism. The super-powers always did exactly that.

The tallest skyscrapers with the record-breaking prices of penthouses no longer prove success of a nation, neither do the launches of aimless rockets confirm victory, rather signs of blatant defeat of the grassroots functionalities. The old rotten system cannot be modified, as new dawn demands new beginnings, new page; free from fakery, divisive politics and conflict driven economic models.

People do not change, but transform anxiously with opportunities right in front. Incompetence to cope with global age demands is currently a serious global blockade. It's time to awaken hidden and immense potential talents of people resulting in opportunities and charge ahead with rapid transformation. Current models will not. Absence of entrepreneurialism in bureaucracies of the world is the biggest challenge. Public sector transformation via lifelong learning can be a salvage operation. Entrepreneurialism mobilization can overcome such hurdles.

Remember, 100 years ago entrepreneurs were simply jailed, 20 years ago intentionally given bad credit ratings by institutions to stop their business pursuits. Now entrepreneurialism, finally discovered as the solution and making it the most popular political word on election podiums. Entrepreneurialism, when deployed across the nation as a national agenda can make economic recovery a comfortable journey.

Let the arrival of new billion entrepreneurs mature, let the billions unemployed transform into global age players, let the public sector leadership relearn and let the five billion connected alpha dreamers change the world. Do your part with ethics, integrity, tolerance and diversity. Join us.

Your existence as a soul today is already a miracle.

The rest is easy.

Chapter One

The mind is limitless and is hardwired like the open universe,
therefore a focused mind is one of the biggest achievements of life.

Are you an alpha dreamer?

Let's explore a bit; you have all kinds of challenges, big and small problems, on growth, performance, prosperity and on advancements, on leadership and on progress. You have questions; you have answers, you have vision, ideas and game plans. You have fears, but you also have mega inspirations. You are brave and you are marching ahead. You are also seeking special help. You want more. Imagine yourself in top leadership position and suddenly called upon on national agenda for grassroots prosperity and gainful occupation for people in your region, what will be your first top three action plans? Kindly hold this thought for a minute. Let's explore more.

To appreciate the finer details of these concepts, it's critical to relate these questions to some of your typical challenges you are facing today. You, your teams and your organization are facing complex situations right now. Irrespective of where you are in the world or the size or type of the venture you face right now, you are passing through the eye of the needle.

You are aware of the storms. You are aware of the warning signs.

"The Boardroom debates and discussions are becoming gibberish. The clarity of vision is being challenged; the meaning of leadership is in chaos; productivity and performance have become noises of confusion and profitability issues are like screams of desperations. Local, national or global scale survival is in a crisis, without understanding of global scale technology down-streaming. There are multiple directions, which itself a whole new threat."

The world is going nowhere

It is stuck in the deep mud of debt, smokes of fake GDP figures, false unemployment numbers, and fires of fake news and storms of fake wars. The current leadership of the world's super-power to micro-power nations are mostly in a downward spiral. The only thing keeping them going is the art of 'make believe' solutions and teleprompter knowledge. The digital renaissance has now equalized the powers of global political elitism, balanced with the power of prosperity information and adjusted global public opinion making political shenanigans more visible and cries of citizenry more audible. Is there a solution to fix this? No, there is not. The current methodologies being implemented as turnaround options are mostly hallucinations. Is it time for war? The same incompetent global punditry that created this mess believes it so. Is there a better solution? Yes, there is.

Today, mankind is in trouble and mankind's problem can only be fixed by mankind's' rules. The biggest and single most important part of mankind is the human brain. There is nothing else like this in the universe. Can we find solutions here? Yes, we can.

Few options are available. Self-learning to achieve superior performance and acquire global age skills. Entrepreneurial transformation to uplift organizations to meet global age performance. National mobilizations of entrepreneurialism to solve local grassroots prosperity.

Each aspect is explained in detail in the following chapters. First item, creating the mental capacity to understand and appreciate global age demands.

The cathedrals of the mind

Should we just ignore all of our out of body experiences of enlightenment? A platform for possible solutions. Creating change, making a difference and actually implementing solutions is a special process, it is an organized effort that will obtain success in altering the state of dissatisfaction, confusion, chaos and disfunctions. Through a series of exercises and implementation of directed thought processes, it may bring order to the chaos, crystallization of the dreams be it in the personal achievement's realm, organizational environments, the prosperity creation mandates of a nation, or the international outlook on the state of the world. For those at any level, who are absolutely fed-up with the current issues, for those who are seeking solutions, major change and solutions, there is a way. The following exercise is at the helm of the thinking process which will ultimately lead to better performances:

The following exercise is only for those who are absolutely fed-up with the current surroundings and are seeking major change; Close your eyes and imagine that your mind is divided into four sections; each a super gigantic dome. Now let's go and fly inside.

When imagination gets space to fly around; achieving a conscious understanding of the current and immediate positioning; in other words, obtaining awareness of our mental existence, realities, challenges and hidden solutions, a quest for enlightenment, imagine four domes.

Earthly cognitions: this is the first dome; this is where we live; where our immediate surroundings have allowed us to become subjected to our own routines which control us; we are a product of our own knowledge and inventions. This is where we deal with issues like, where we live, work, play, socialize culturize or nationalize. This is where we face our daily challenges based on who we are, where we come from, what we do and why. This is where we are subjected to all of the many varieties of daily grinds, routines and structures. We are inundated with chores, tasks, procedures, and these demands create smooth or out of control living patterns. This is where we try to understand most of our problems based on our own understanding and where we occasionally find answers. Struggling and coping with issues can have side effects on our health, personality and prosperity. Accepting the burdens of daily realities can shut down our own mental faculties and at times prohibit new ideas for the mind to grow. This massive space to float around with our imagination sometime may feel like a lush garden to dance with joy or a barbwire prison with guards. Suddenly, clarity may occur with a realization in knowing that having blindly followed all the old traditional rules what are the hidden and most powerful intuitive strengths that were never utilized.

Blindly following all the old traditional rituals, custom and procures does not keep our legacy alive but sometimes becomes the proof that the old practitioners were already mentally dead. We simply follow routines and accept unquestionably whatever is offered comes from a long traditional perspective? There are hidden values in the traditions but far more valuable is the desire to explore. Refusal to blindly accept these conditions, for whatever reason, only activate our imagination provided it is wired to dream on a key agenda and with clarity. The rate of refusal to the daily grind is directly proportioned to increased imagination. This process is not about noticing flaws but carefully self-discovering our own limitations and finding ways to dramatically expand and improve them. The more uncomfortable we are with our surroundings the more, fuel we get to kindle our imagination.

During the last millennia, the majority of earth-shattering personalities who altered our way of life were totally disgusted with their immediate, internal and external environments. They boldly rejected their disposition, and they boosted their imagination, fought with brand new ideas and changed and brought massive progress. Here the process may lead you to become an authority on yourself. Guide you to develop logical rational thinking and become a person with superior performance. Show you to become a new warrior to deal with our own global-age challenges?

Suggestions: listing all your big and small problems and daily monitoring such large lists will start showing alternate solutions. The regular updating of the list in micro details becomes a reality check to allow advance thinking and ideas.

The secrets; You may reject your surrounding in any way you wish, but you don't do it with anger. Anger is your enemy; do not confront your dedicated and highly focused march with anger. Go forward with humility; after all these surroundings have helped you to reach where you are today with both mental and physical preparedness. Only upon acknowledging the lack of certain skills will your mind and body open to receive new energies, enlightenments and embrace new knowledge and skills. Every moment of life, good or bad helps you; every day is a sum of experiences and learning of new things. Nothing is wasted. You may reflect at the absurdity and stupidity of your surroundings, but for you to have a healthy and positive conversation with your mind it will only happen when you have discovered better thinking, innovations and new options. Whatever you may call dysfunctionalities of your surroundings can only be classified as such only when you have created a better vision and deeper understanding filled with solid solutions. Otherwise all these frustrations will only sound as excuses. To reject surroundings demands deeper analysis and specific alternates with deliverable game plans. Embrace hostility and brutal circumstances as constant learning grounds for advancements.

The lack of light in caves forced mankind to advance and come out of darkness. All was done in step by step advancements, based on the deployment of applications and mobilized as invented options. Simple rejection in order to stay quiet and avoid debates will get you nowhere. Lingering in depressions is no progress. Today's working societies of the world are intensely occupied with blaming their surrounding but with little or nothing offered as new solutions for advancements. Smile more;

19

complain less; imagine hard and communicate with specific advancement strategies. We grow in tough situations; we only become stronger with experiences. Complaints are not the bridges to advancements, solution and deployments are.

Now, let's assume you recognize such a difficult and complicated place and can relate all that to your own and immediate realities. Only after you have a good dialogue with your mind, can you strive to identify each of the four spaces of your intellectual living and explore how the cathedrals of the mind have provided four special domes.

Celestial heights: this is the second dome; this is where we fly on the wings of our imagination; this is where your imagination will allow you to fly around in all directions at all speed. Imagination is a dream for the awakened. Planned imagination is for the enlightened. Structured and well-defined imagination is the visualization of early reality. Executable imagination is where ideas start turning into real life happenings. This is where your mind is challenged to prove your depth of self-discovery, talents and enlightenment. The mind can create concepts in great details, like take ordinary sugar, turn it into specially flavored wrapped candy, and deliver it via global franchise system to every shopping mall in the world, or deliver million seeds on thousands of acres in symmetrical fashion via 100 drones. Understanding of such celestial powers demands special emotional stamina in order to balance controlled creativity.

In each Olympic Games, spanning over last 100 years, there are two most painful moments for athletes and for their nations, firstly, coming 4th because they missed the medal by a fraction and secondly winning a silver medal because they missed the gold. After all the agony, the world most skillful athletes and their special coaches dive into highly unique processes to recover back their stamina and performances for the next games, not by intensifying or doubling their training routines, but by relaxing and going through intense mental exercise to imagine victory and call upon body to realign muscles and retrain their body to understand how superior performances measured in fraction of seconds work. Mind retrains muscles and body in an attempt to become number one in the world. The is an amazing discipline. Mind stays in the driver seat.

Imagination is the least used facility in our daily lives because we pretend, we are busy. We are trapped by social media to observe others rather than being internally focused on our own imaginary paths and our own challenges that would bring amazing ideas into realities. From the early start family and education restricted much of our imaginary thinking and now the Internet and social media has impacted the corporate culture of the world, and has brought human talent and imagination to a standstill. Human productivity and performance now a big challenge across the world.

Suggestions: rough sketches, blueprints and schedules are all important here, used as master plans under study, ensure confident developments and advancements.

Incomprehensible realms: this is the third dome; this is where our unknowns are hidden; this is where we search without knowing what we are looking for. Our world was discovered during the last few millennia and we have only scratched the surface of it and have no idea why our earth, like a dust particle blown in the wind storm of galaxies. The mind is curious and not scared of darkness; however, it needs to venture out in the unknown where curiosity forces to change and meets solutions and alternates. Whatever is known today came out of our curiosity; whatever is still unknown out there is hidden behind the walls of curiosity. This dome is where all discoveries and intuitive thinking open doors and bring new concepts. Once the imagination gets unlimited free space, and once the earthly boredom is ignored, the unexplained gets explained. This where we try our odd and new things and which upon success get called entrepreneurial streaks, and this is how we become champions. All over the world greatest entrepreneurs had no idea of what they were capable of until they did their first venture. We are all born entrepreneurs divided into ones already discovered and others still untapped. Which one are you?

Suggestions; list all the impossibilities, break them into small pieces, all the difficult and complex tasks and force all issues in a jambalaya and never worry about the outcome. Finally, some flash of light will occur.

Will this work wonders for you, depends on your effort, however by having allowed our minds to stretch and reaching outside the boundaries of impossibilities, we have created another dimension, a space where we can place our dreams and our ideas, our thoughts and plans, and we accept that they are almost attainable, and we can build? We are dreamers

Architectural sensibility: this is the fourth dome; here we design with mastery, balance and quality. Within this dome is where we take new ideas and create them into global realities; this is where we define new ideas, laws, rules and logic surrounding it, the center of its gravity. From Adam's apple to Newton's laws or to Job's creations, all these apples were subjected to gravity, each with its own unique processes and methodologies. The mind is very capable of creating structured balance, innovative designs and its required exploratory processes reaching a solid purpose. This is where the mind gets ready to deploy architectural thinking in order to frame unexplored creations and to slowly bring them to new realities. Mankind is already hardwired to constantly create better living and prosperity. Today the world's most expensive real estate stands were caves dwelling several millennia ago were the lifestyles. Mankind has the brain and it finds creative solutions. Mankind is hard-wired for advancement. This is also how in the ancient age, without any communication, identical Pyramids were built around the world. This is how mankind learned to speak no matter what they did or where they were located in the world, each built their own language knowledge. Now get ready and witness around the world, how Silicon Valleys of all kinds and Bollywoods of all sorts are popping up in 200 cultures and languages. Individuals are creating the unthinkable in places considered impossible. The mind is the ultimate driver. It can do anything.

Suggestions; draw out full and detailed structures, procedures and binders and test all aspects, as ideas and solutions are useless without full and micro-detailed execution.

If done properly and as your imagination filters out the very best of the pathways, solutions, ideas and extreme innovative thinking. At this point and upon such discoveries, this is ow you gain the passage to the next dome of architectural challenges, form tightrope walking to trapeze flying; you will find the right balance and the proper structure you need for your new idea, because this is your private and very deluxe sandbox where you can play with new ideas. Depending on the right conditions, within weeks you may become the best on your floor; within months best in your corporate tower; within years you can be the best in the nation or the world. It's all about you, your brain, your well-defined spaces that will allow your mind to work and relentless desire to become a superior performer. Rest is easy. Now, can your mind see the four very large domes? Relax, it will.

Ready for a Test Flight

If you feel overly-compressed with boredom of chores and undesirable mandates that absolutely frustrate you to points of no returns, you may need to ask your mind to leave your current dome of daily realities, then enter into the new dome of celestial heights where your mind and imagination fly all around seeking new solutions. Here, any advancement will automatically lead you to the other dome of incomprehensible spaces where like mazes and puzzles you will. These self-learning may take months or years but can be tried anytime, anywhere, in our own universe of your imaginations and goals and desires. It's you and your dreams taking shape into realities. It is fun. How to recognize specific symptoms during any venture or enterprise expansion and how to mobilize steady progressions.

The typical symptoms

There are very common-symptoms, like stress, fear, discomfort, lack of motivation, lack of sleep, lack of energy, all these symptoms felt by all, from boardrooms to office and factory floors, from every corner of the office, every floor of the entire corporate towers and also in all of the towers of any nation. Little or nothing is being done on these issues at the organizational level, because so often nothing seems to work and now people are expected to have stamina to cope with them at varying degrees of intensity. There are also some specific-symptoms such as the compulsory behavior of becoming overly-busy, non-stop talking, cover-ups lying or misinformation that prohibits progress. All of these are direct effects of prolonged frustrations and lack of productivity. There are also the hidden-symptoms such as panic attacks, anxiety moments, depression and addictions, and these become destructive forces and cripple lifelong performances.

Two questions: First, is organizational misbehavior becoming that bad? And second, is leadership unable to solve such lingering issues. In broad strokes, the answers to both are yes. Today all of these symptoms at varying degrees of intensities are accepted as a normal nature of the beast. Everyone is trying for betterment but nothing magical is being achieved.

An enterprise is driven not by muscle power but mental power. Entrepreneurial problems are all mental and organization performance is all about optimized performance and that performance is all about self-discovery in order to be able to manage global age skills…it's all about mental performance and self-discovered stamina.

Beyond 2020 delivering an idea on a grand scale of managing performance of an enterprise is no longer an educated guess; it's hardcore global age entrepreneurial maneuver and no longer children's play.

The calendar dependency to common symptoms

Should we just ignore our daily symptoms of imbalances and close doors on possible alternates? By and large, enterprises run on tight calendars, daily checklists, weekly updates, quarterly results, annual budgets and bonuses. Here are frequently repeated symptoms haunting the elite cadre all over the world.

The Monday Blues: the opening of the Pandora's box, such as, there is nothing new in the yearlong innovation exercise, the costs are over-budget, the competition just pulled a fast one, the delivery dates are over stretched, the leadership is under the desk, the vision under the carpet, the morals out of the door.

The Tuesday Tangos: the production was overly creative, color post-it tabs dominate all white walls, the new creative culture meets the real factory floors, fancy lingo turns into shop-talk, will the teams dance together, absence of global age skills make the tango off-beat.

The Wednesday's Weddings: the two underperforming products are engaged, two leadership-less divisions married, two teams working on the same floor get new titles and new organigrams without new directions or mandates, prolonged agony calls for prenups.

The Thursdays Thrills; new rebranding announced, new makeover accomplished, new sing-songs start, new slogan on the walls, new mission statements memorized, customers confused, consumer mesmerized, all goes north, all sales go south. Lack of clues.

The Friday Falls: more new products from competitors, new market shift now visible, leadership wants a major push, teams are confused, lack of skills obvious, nothing is ready, no one knows, silent in boardroom, vision missing.

The Saturday Slips; the annual trade show stall missed the marketing brochures, the products shipped in wrong language, the call center is overloaded, the customers are upset, the paperless process failed, media is calling.

The Sunday Surprises; new management agenda rolls out, new launches rolled out, all consultants argue and big firm accountants start cost-cutting and head chopping, something new has to happen, time to beg, borrow or steal, clocks get frozen, promise of a brand-new fresh start of Monday.

Discovering cognitive blind spots

The art of discovering your own cognitive blind spots; You may or may not spot your own cognitive blind spots, but you are faced with them every day. The majority of our daily encounters have blind spots and if we are not aware of these blind spots, each and every time we will miss something. The look of a person, a key word during a discussion, the response from the audience, the color of light at an intersection, the sudden turn, a swift angle, the contents while flipping a magazine, the punch line or a word in these last few lines. These can all be blind spots.

This is, of course, is a defensive mechanism of our mind, which keeps us from noticing very small detail or remembering every single make of car on a highway. But when it comes to key issues directly related to our key points of required observations, we sometime discover these blind spots in our afterthoughts. Our eyes are smartly connected with our brain and all our senses are in harmony with our body, but just like an optical illusion, where no matter how much we force our self, we still cannot decipher the illusionary image. In our daily lives, we have a constant flow of puzzling and mesmerizing situations where our senses fail us. Sometime we do not see the color, perspective, size, balance or trajectory and either they fall into a blind spot or we just believe in what's in front of us as a simple view. Once again, a deeper study of the subject is mandatory. Some people are color blind and have difficulty deciphering the traffic lights; we are all deaf, mute and blind to some degree and still do not understand all colors, sounds and our own enunciations. We observe with curiosity, but we also shut out and lose out in our own blind spots.

This is how we go on our journeys. This is how we develop better and sharper senses. This is how we become better observers, and it's always good to know what we are capable of. Now sit calmly in a garden and just observe.

Top ten building strategies

To build great new ideas, how to use such powerful tools to create balanced structure. Each topic is discussed in great detail in various chapters.

Should we avoid deep diving into freely available technologies?

Strategy One: Technocalamity:

Definition: When the overflow of free technology drowns old establishments and allows new young ones to become iconic leaders.

Usage: to build any new idea demands solid understanding of technology that can be used throughout the concepts with an architectural sense of structure and balance in order to allow technological hold on all functions from top to bottom of the enterprise.

Symptoms: Long innovative process are now failing on commercialization; things have moved into unknown; new thinking is required; skill gaps are visible; finger pointing and panicky cost-cutting is the new rule. New technologies are drowning old thinking. What is next?

Should we become overly content with whatever quality we produce?

Strategy Two: Age of abundance:

Definition: Age of Abundance has followed the age of curiosity and scarcity; we are in the age of abundance, where for every great idea, we have thousands of better ones.

Usage: build any new idea with extreme uniqueness and high value design.

Symptoms: PR, promotional campaigns are up but sales are down; competition has better, faster, cheaper options; the race is being lost; victory is hidden in other brand-new strategies; vision is being challenged, and the fog of confusion is cutting profits.

Should we only regard our hardware and factories as our only assets?

Strategy Three: Soft-power-assets management:

Definition: Soft-power assets are invisible assets such as vision, imagination and creative entrepreneurial skills.

Usage: build with creativity and wild imagination, like using steel and cement to hold a skyscraper.

Symptoms: Massive structural sets up now appear outdated, no new options, formulations and methodologies now appear liabilities, constant cost cutting will undermine stability, massive shift is new skills and strategies a must.

Should we accept our current speed of progress as top standard?

Strategy Four: Equation 365=365:

Definition: how to achieve in 365 hours what we are conditioned to achieve in 365 days.

Usage: create high speed performance by new thinking of time and optimization, like high speed elevators work in skyscrapers.

Symptoms: For every new thrust in markets competition, the markets are always few steps ahead; long cycles of innovative thinking are hurting the organization; traditionally sluggish operation needs new definitions and new behavior to survive

Should we be happily satisfied in a 9-5 working model?

Strategy Five: Live 24x7x365:

Definition: how to create around the clock 24x7x365 organizational culture for global accessibility?

Usage: expand with new global age access and massive communication.

Symptoms: Local markets peaked, organizations cannot open dozens of new global age markets; retraining of the frontline delayed; processing of international business a nightmare, globally accessibility in crisis.

Should we do nothing to improve our future?

Strategy Six: Alpha dreamers:

Definition: The five billion connected dreamers who will change the world.

Usage: Understanding the rise of alpha dreamers as a new world opens.

Symptoms: lack of Intellectualization of the organization on deep and precise understanding of the customers at large; new alliances; new funding; lack of quality contents; right language; better and smarter management.

Should we avoid any additional complex thinking models?

Strategy Seven: Quadrability formation:

Definition: mastery of four-dimensional thinking styles and multidirectional advancements.

Usage: how to create four times the productivity, four times the performance and four times the profitability.

Symptoms: Standstill no-action mode; Silence and do not rock the boat mentality; Silos and disconnections of all complex issues; critical need for interactive and bold dialogue to demonstrate consensus, while improving multidimensional thinking and execution

Should we only live on a day-to-day business planning model?

Strategy Eight: The global age:

Definitions: The global age is a post e-commerce cultural and entrepreneurial shift.

Usage: acquiring trend-hunting mastery, when growth is absent; understanding global age and open new markets.

Symptoms: Management has little or no ideas on the top trends forcing the industry; lack of superiority of knowledge, decision making and execution; lack of understanding of the global age, and lack of thought leadership on market differentiation

Should we only be happy with our own prosperity and not care about others?

Strategy Nine: Grassroots prosperity:

Definition: how to help local-national-global landscape at the grassroots level.

Usage: Social responsibility to create local grassroots prosperity,

Symptoms: lack of social responsibility and knowledge on how to mobilize local or regional programs to help the community grow; lack of contents to make Cabinet level presentations and stand up as a leader

Should we only target our local customer base and ignore the world?

Strategy Ten: Image supremacy protocols:

Definition: mastery of global image positioning.

Usage: how to lead across national and global marketplace creating intellectual property assets.

Symptoms: Lack of understanding of superiority of image and identity in the global marketplace and extreme value creation and image generation protocols, being stuck in decades old logo-slogan mentality

The above ten top critical components to provide wings to any great iconic ideas are explained in great details in the following chapters.

Each of the above item is covered in details in the following chapters.

Advanced Cognitions

No paper and pencil required: Visualize and imagine your entire enterprise or your new entrepreneurial idea; analyze it from top to bottom, all the hard and soft structures it occupies, the building, factories, warehouses, trucks and machineries, the pathways, the talented people, floors and elevators, the water coolers and corner-offices, the cafeterias and parking lots. Now, hold this entire structure in your imagination as if it was all in front of you as a fully functional three-dimensional reality. Now go inside to each key touch points of the main operations where your goods and services start into action, do the full loop from start to finish; step by step go over all the key processes till all such processes are satisfactorily complied and final results delivered to the end user, the customer. Once fully figured out, you are now ready to move to the next stage. In this next stage, now multiply in size and volume this visualized concept and structure by a hundred times, this will suddenly create a gigantic, monstrous looking empire right in front of you, now, once again, visualize all the big and small structures and operational flows, now re-imagine how the operation will unfold and how the production or services will flow to achieve the highest speed, quality, performance and profitability. Here, once again, you carefully visualize all the inter-flows and connecting of dots to move goods or services from point A to Z. At this stage your new difficult challenge is to isolate the entire flow of production while step by step erasing all the hard structure, the building, offices, floors, and people. What's left is a visualized schematic rendering of your core delivery and processing of your goods and services all visible only in your mind. A highly workable and efficient flow chart, without people and building structures. If you can do this you are already a very high-quality senior leadership potential

Now, we start the hard part; start re-arranging the entire work flow based on your knowledge, intuitions, talents, imagination and your wisdom, by process of elimination, you will design better pathways, better floor set up and smarter layouts to transform this humongous organization into a highly streamlined functioning enterprise. Once you have comfortably done this, once again, you only save the operational flows and eliminate the entire hard structures around. Leaving you with a brand-new schematic rendering with very thoughtful and with improved and different flows and outcomes. If you can do this you are already an amazing visionary leader. Now, moving to the more advanced part, first achieve a comfort level of all this, depending on your skills, this may take a day or a full year of practice to arrive at such levels. Now compress this flow from 100 times bigger to the original 1% size where you started from; now that the entire flow has so dramatically changed and schematics start looking so different, start layering to this flow a different brand-new re-dressing with the right styles and shapes, buildings, offices, floors and now you will need special teams and talented people. An amazing shift of thinking has already taken place. Series of brand-new observations may open new alternates. This is high level work if done carefully and properly. Entrepreneurs thrive is this space, constantly visualizing, shrinking and enlarging their complex innovative ideas and their relative flow charts, changing schematics upside down and managing trainloads of people all the time resulting in high quality well thought out answers with high quality deliberations fine-tuned to fit any 24x7x365 access demands. That's why entrepreneurs appear as wizards in meetings, this is how they acquire authoritative knowledge, all tabled in boardrooms and labeled as gutsy wisdom at extremely difficult crossroads. This is how many dozens of such idea building and execution scenarios are living in their minds most of the time. That's why their work is not funding dependent it's all about fine tuning ideas to meticulous perfection so they become magnets to funding. This is how they live in unimaginable spaces of new ideas, sequenced to optimize the minimum of resources for maximum returns and ready with executable blueprints. That's why entrepreneurs are confidently ahead of the game. Entrepreneurs discover this all by themselves but only at their first attempts, as before such activity they have no idea about their hidden talents, in time with trials and errors they acquire mastery, this is when others start labeling them as crazy entrepreneurs. If you comfortably reach this point try these exercises on a few bold and impossible projects and you will be pleasantly surprised at your own hidden talents. You will realize that solutions and answers are automatically coming to surface. Lifelong learning and working with mind will become an amazing journey.

Just, imagine, visualize and create your own future.

Chapter Two

After crossing over the horizon, you may see the real new world

Five billion dreamers changing the world

Today, a common person on any street of the world is very often more knowledgeable on truth than their own governments; constant access to live information with accuracy deciphering truth from fakery is training the new global age generations. Therefore, these well-connected five billion people of the world are the Alpha-dreamers. They are very capable of dreaming a better future, because they are willing to listen, discuss, improve and solve problems for humankind via collaborative synthesizim.

They are young and old, big or small; they represent us all. They are from different genders, races, cultures, nationalities and whether rich or poor, employed or unemployed, they are all asking questions. They are surrounded by deep silence and asking for intelligent debates. They are creating new survival strategies and chasing the truth. They will dream of a better future, they know a bit more about each other, because never before has there ever existed such a large global mindshare. They are the world's largest group of constantly connected; they are a silent mindshare and the silent voice of our future. Inaudible still to media and political leadership and they will be the most powerful influencers as the global age takes over. After two millenniums, it is time for the Third Millennia to dream better and create better realities.

Dreams lay the foundations for upcoming realities.
Dreams and decisions with execution become realities.
Dreamers with imaginations develop vision and ideas.
Dreamers see things that others miss.

Looking at today's realities, how far will our civilization go when citizens have unlimited printed money to feel rich, a gun to play mighty, drugs to play zombie, and where perpetual chaos of bigotry is accepted as high-society fashionable living and dogmatic culture as new intellectualism.

Alpha dreamers can find better solutions and will build better sustainable models in order for the world to survive. They have two options; either they will just survive or they will emerge with commitment to build a better world. How will all this unfold?

The future of humankind is mental-power driven as muscle-power which will be transferred to machines and technology and as we advance, mental-power will be forced to improve and invent a new higher class of performance while muscle-power will be encouraged to be left for health improvement of the mental-power and overall body, machines will turn into robots and technology into constantly live virtual globally connected landscape.

Every person on earth has mental powers, we were simply trained to not use them, forced to follow a special agenda-centric curriculum designed to make us deaf and blind with Babble

Humankind was repeatedly rejected over quick gains and special interests.

We must learn to unlearn; we must learn to relearn, all in order to see with our minds and not just with our eyes; we must relearn to hear with our consciousness and not just with ears, and not laugh at the world as an obscene-comedy act but embrace it with our hearts and smile with our brains because its natural beauty and harmony will guide us.

The future is all about letting our ideas fly in cathedrals of our own conscious imagination where unlimited knowledge is only a click away, and unlimited global access to five billion Alpha dreamers making pathways to better prosperity surrounds us. The future is what we make of it today, while the rest is just fake news and fake agendas.

Dreamers can see this

The mind has proven its travel throughout mankind, from caves to Mars.

The journey of mind; a tireless, ageless, wanderer, mind is your number one and most precious asset in the world, and never let anybody tell you differently. Realization and mastery of your own craft will allow adventurous travels of your mind and enable it to cross the new global shifts towards new horizons, where a brighter and greener world waits for you. This journey will only be possible if your mind is your friend and ready to travel. Remember, the new world no longer needs your body to sit on chairs, elbows to lean on desks, eyes to watch the clock or fingers to type. Now, all is needed is your mind. What is needed now is smart global age friendly minds, to wander and roam. But why?

Let's ask some more difficult questions, let's look at the big picture in precise details so other issues will all become clearer.

Four enlightenments

Four critical types of personal enlightenments needed to fix the future. Explained in details in the following chapters.

Self-Discovery; close your eyes and discover your hidden talents, create supreme performance and become a global age thinker. This will lead to;

Enterprising Journeys; open your eyes and study the global age and indulge at the enterprise level, build and create massive growth. Do something phenomenal. This will lead to;

Grassroots Prosperity; lead by example, deploy and create grassroots prosperity, improve surroundings, help teams, share knowledge and create extreme value. This will lead to;

National Mobilization; share your authoritative command and knowledge, mobilize and help your own nation and make sure it is moving in the right direction, assist in boosting the national economy. A better future arrives.

Super-power-nations balanced against with micro-power-nations

When Super power nations start losing their powers to fix the entire world, micro power nations can start contributing to mankind problems. Success is not the overly hedged fake economy rather global harmony, diversity and human development. Can nations ever ignore the hidden talents of their citizenry? Can leadership ever fail to demonstrate their superior skills to help and mobilizes small and medium size business across the nation? Can political agenda ever fail to prioritize continuous self-learning as a way to foster occupational superiority for the nation?

Chapter Three

Unimaginable new destinations require untraveled new roads

Marathons of exportability

As leaders responsible for prosperity should we ignore our thousands or millions of small medium businesses? Can we just ignore all small medium trade organizations across the nation, successful and mandated to foster grassroots prosperity but let them continue operating on the same behind the times thinking and decades old style performances? Should we just avoid serious debates, discussions on conflicting points of views on global age commerce? Should we just stay mum and quiet on all grassroots prosperity execution styles and prosperity affairs?

Creating marathons of exportability & innovative excellence. There are programs and solutions which are resoundingly different and extremely novel and focuses on combative, tactical formats delivered exclusively in powerful and dramatically engaging styles to owners and founders of small and midsize enterprises. Such concepts are deluxe integration of rich contents and global experiences that creates positive impact within the enterprise. Around the world, political leadership blinded by old systems do not have the organizational capacity to fathom such revolutionary thinking, otherwise thy would done these decades ago.

The Five Pillars of Global-Age Transformation: Program brings a new global age philosophy, new avenues of thinking and execution, and train as follows;

Global Age Exportability: What's really stopping a high potential enterprise from expanding to 100-200 countries?

Global Age Thinking: What will it take to re-organize and operate as a multinational organization with little or no extra costs?

Global Age Modeling: How to optimize and integrate soft power assets with currently available hard asset centricity.

Global Age Execution: How to train yourself to achieve what normally takes 365 normal days to do it in only 365 dramatic hours.

Global Age Presence: How to bring the Image Supremacy of innovative excellence in a big triumph.

Global Age Prosperity: How to become a magnet of prosperity with new revenues, new funding, and new alliances

These deployment ready programs can transform 1000 to 10,000 local small and midsize businesses in any sector or region to become global-age players. This can only be achieved with sophisticated delivery system of transformational debates, entrepreneurial strategies and expert discussions with pragmatic solutions critical to expansion realities on the creation of grassroots prosperity by mobilizing enterprise owners. Creation of local prosperity nation by nation will save the mankind from the current chaos.

To clarify any lingering confusion, these programs and thinking are not only very deluxe program but also categorically not to be confused with traditional university and academic education classes, online courses or startup and incubator events. This program different and extremely novel and focused on combative, tactical formats delivered exclusively in powerful and dramatically engaging styles to owners, founders and job-creators.

Exclusive Benefits to Participating Nations: They help showcase national entrepreneurial mobilization of enterprise wide performances. They blend real pragmatism with national themes via solid deliverable platform. National role encourages major trade associations to also join the charge and shine. These programs create mobilization readiness. Assists a nation to identify from 1000 to 10,000 high potential small enterprises for global age expansion. Assist creating major agenda contents on Global Age National Entrepreneurialism & Exportability. Assist in selection of 100 plus Key high-profile candidates for various TV debates and discussions. Such programs improve current status of the current national issues, like: Nations are already flooded with massive innovations, but lack massive commercialization. Nations have over certifications and degrees but seriously lack business directions. Nations have empty incubators and exhausted accelerators like real estate projects. Nations have economic development programs but often without mega punch. Nations have an attractive message and political platform and wake-up call for smart nations.

Are the current methodologies of creating economic prosperity in your vertical sector acceptable? Will you stop an all-out entrepreneurial driven economic turnaround? Do you believe your national leadership is fully conversant with national mobilization of entrepreneurialism protocols? Do you think this is what they are teaching at universities of the world on entrepreneurialism? This high-level thinking and debates create alternates to the following national difficulties.

Top ten most difficult national transformational challenges:

Why is Entrepreneurialism taught in classrooms? Armies are not, they are in tactical combats.

Why is the global age connected society of Alpha-dreamers being ignored? They are over two billion talented assets who are ready and willing to help make smart decisions.

Why is Technocalamity, the free overflow of technology so feared? It is altering business landscape.

Why is the deployment of soft power asset management so foreign and why hard power asset is thinking still the driving force in organizations and governments? Why do we refuse new thinking?

Why will population rich nations take over knowledge rich nations? Nations are getting confused over excessive knowledge and no growth over large population and massive activity.

Why are national innovation and incubation mantras single day photo-ops? How much longer will organizations and nations continue this nonproductive PR practices?

Why are super power nations challenged by micro-power-nations who are quadrupling exportability?

Why are typical conference models becoming obsolete? Now, push button global thought leadership access is available.

Why is global collaborative synthesizim so misunderstood? Old thinking lacks global age understanding.

Why are diversity, entrepreneurialism and women power considered threat? There is a lack of global age wisdom.

These ideas further assist with the top five most critical national performance challenges:

How can Trade Associations become 24x7x365 alive high-performance global marketing machines?

How can Awards and Annual events become 24x7x365 high quality deliverers of 365 days of programs?

How can houses of trade and Chambers of Commerce become 24x7x365 value with 365 days of global programming?

How can Export development hunting operate at 24x7x365 high value global performance levels

How can Government's economic programs become 24x7x365 superior command and control

The time to change has already passed, and the time to mobilize and revolutionize has started.
Why is soft power asset management so foreign to hard asset thinking?
Why is there a lack of knowledge on soft power assets?
Why are super-power-nations challenged by micro-power-nations?
Quadrupling exportability will be the answer for progress.
Why is global collaborative synthesizim so misunderstood?
There is a huge lack of global age understanding.
Why are diversity, entrepreneurialism and women power considered threats? There is a lack of wisdom about how diversity strengthens decision making.

What's stopping the steady continuous flow of pragmatic contents and workable ideas?

Why can't houses of trade and chambers prove 24x7x365 value with 365 days of global programming?

What is stopping the massive creation of global bounce of leads and opportunities in real time?

Why can't Export development hunting groups operate on a 24x7x365 basis with high value global performance levels?

What is stopping sophisticated large live data bases from bouncing in real time?

Why can't Government economic programs lead 24x7x365 with superior messages, full control and command?

How can organizations and governments lead by example by creating image supremacy protocols of innovative excellence?

Hard Facts and Warm Realities:

Managing a digital economy of a nation is no different, it's just a very, very large motherboard, basically, many platforms, massive data and all inter-connected with beautiful graphics and friendly pictures to create maximum exposure of their entrepreneurial talents, goods and services to some 200 countries. Not to be confused with current old-style websites and broken links and emails. The social media is great for posting pictures of cakes and silly videos, this is a superior business-to-business sector program for 200 nations of the world. Nations without massive and successful digitally-accessible-economies will have serious consequences and will appear as dark spots on the global maps. Last century, nations without electricity were in darkness, today without hyper-digitalized-midsize economy they are lacking the luminance of mind and prosperity creation knowledge. A new and smart world is awakening right in front of us. Check your binoculars.

Chapter Four

Success at times is failure management;
failure is often a lost battle but not a
lost war, ultimate success is not necessarily winning the war,
success is more about understanding the battlefield,
as the real victory is hidden outside the war.

Mankind was born entrepreneurial

That's why we came out of caves. Fragmentation of our mankind came with the industrial age, boundaries and restrictions, we got divided and segregated, purged and isolated. With artificial intelligence technologies and global connectives, instant translations we have options to reunite as one mind as one common cause to save and protect mankind. In this pursuit of common mindshare and open dialogue to sort out conflicts the lingering doctrine that prefers conflicts over dialogue should be banned.

Do not force change on others, give them light so they will find their own way. Do not change the world, just change yourself.

The advancement of mankind via inequality is wrong alignment. Harmony, diversity and equality creating local grassroots prosperity is the natural growth. The parasites of fakery are the diseases of today in need of cure.

In absence of politically driven solutions, leadership clarity on the global crisis of local grassroots prosperity can now only be fixed by entrepreneurialism. How?

Entrepreneurialization of a nation

How will Entrepreneurialization of a nation work? Master blueprints: The understanding on the differentiation between fake entrepreneurialism and real true entrepreneurialism is critically essential. Societies will be better served when national leadership and gatekeepers of the grassroots prosperity all acquire a deeper understanding of entrepreneurialism, in all of its shapes, sizes and styles and its progression from early start-up and out box thinking to all the way to earth-shattering life altering global phenomenon. Here are multi-layered issues and entrepreneurial wisdom for the global age and its transformation via self-discovery and self-optimization. It's important to have a big overview and a global age perspective

FACT:
By 2020, India, China will add one billion new entrepreneurs.
Who are they and how fast are they growing?
Where do they come from and where are they headed?
How systematically were they transformed into entrepreneurs?
How are they multiplying on technology platforms with wings of progress? How will they fly and where will they land and what will they hatch and what should national leaderships plan today on such mobilizations?

Why nations should plan open policy to allow thousands or million entrepreneurs to land and help lead economic-revival-strategies and why nations should demonstrate thought leadership to move forward?

To understand big picture, we must redefine today's realties. These revelations are critical for soft-power-centric smart entrepreneurial nations of the global age, as the rest will stay stagnant and trapped in irrelevant competencies.

Redefinitions of Work Space: when office-less-office, start leaving buildings, downtowns and corporate hierarchies morphs, impacting economies, with cities dwindling and suburbia blooming

Redefinitions of Work: when work is universally mobile and workers are free in their habitats, work finds and arrives, no 9-5 chase, impacting daily living, new living styles and new intellectualism emerge

Redefinitions of Management: when free technologies replace senior and middle management and impact with new realities and social adjustments for hyper productive inter-connected age

Redefinitions of Time: when real time 24x7x365 live culture overtakes old style timelines and calendars are lost, new occupations emerge, professional hobbies and nouveau entrepreneurialism rise

Overview: It's no longer important which economic model you support, which super power you endorse, or to which nation you belong. The proof of decimated policies lingers behind fake economies, fake data and fake news and all of this is enough to recognize that the world is in the eye of an economic storm. We are in the vortex, whirling around totally uncontrolled and now it's time to rebuild strengths and relearn ways to deal with the real truth.

As a counter balance to hologramic economies, stagnation and deep silence the "National Entrepreneurialization of a Country" now becomes an economic survival strategy that is slowly being deployed among smart nations.

Redefinitions of Collaborative Synthesizim: As China, USA and India are the world's most important economies for open and global trade, this CHINDUSA triangulation will strangle its weakest link. The other 100 micro-power-nations, armed with new platforms will start enjoying borderless new markets.

Redefinitions of Entrepreneurial Immigration: Now the USA is considering talent-based immigration over lottery based annual quotas. How many other smart nations are now open to this sophisticated entrepreneurial game? Nouveau Entrepreneurialism has prosperity as its prime objective; it is borderless, universally diverse and tolerant. This is a hidden game changer.

Redefinitions of Super-Data-Controls: Whose data is it in the first place? What data is merging? Data is borderless; artificial intelligence is also borderless and smart enough to seep through walls and spread it power and access around the globe. The new global standards will drive data, which in turn will drive trade flows and economic powers.

Deniers should study the cavemen. Why were they shown no mercy?

Power Questions: The world of Nicolo Machiavelli and his untitled book, later named The Prince, became the most popular recipe on strategy and became the bedside reference cookbook for the world's greatest political leaders. During the last 500 years it was perhaps the most obediently followed "how to" manual on the achievement of materialism by whatever means. Where have all these leaders gone? Have they just disappeared? Absence of wisdom and apologies of their grave mistakes are not unacceptable and their exhumation will also not provide answers. Today, the power house nations have some explaining to do. Their cookbooks of fakery have failed. Machiavellian mentality has damaged mankind. The global age has no space for such thinking. Generations have suffered and it is now left for academia to further ponder on Machiavelli and his cherished wisdom which has resulted in black holes of grassroots economic prosperity.

Mankind demands straight answers.
Mankind seeks new alternatives.
Mankind strives for grassroots prosperity.

Grassroots prosperity

Local grassroots prosperity will eliminate our global chaos, also the reasons for fakery, wars and conflicts.

On this most critical issue, current systems all over the world have failed to varying degrees. Unless these issues are not tackled the global confusion will worsen.

The world like a spinning ball has fallen in a pot of honey, there is so much overly hedged fake economies and fake printed money that it's drowning in a deep and grossly mismanaged financial picture, where only a miniscule percentage controls the remaining mankind. The earth needs to come out of this honey pot clean and sobered up and get into a balanced game. It's not just the honey, it's drowning in the honey, now sting bees are getting ready to attack and misinformation and manipulated data driving the system. A massive wash-up is required.

Super power economies are more aligned to attacking or destroying other economies. They feel this is a prime necessity for their own survival. While new emerging Micro Power Nations are upcoming hungry performers with very special skills and are willing and able to help any small or super power without threatening their base of power. They thrive in mutual collaborative synthesizim. These Micro-Power-Nations may deploy highly selective, well trained and extraordinary strengths and deliver surgical solutions to a mammoth nation and get mutually rewarded. Such specialized capabilities will create universal borderless residencies, merit-based immigration, global friendly fair trading, and unlimited human resources dependent Technocalamity platforms for the new global age world. This new thinking is not the armies invading, but armies of entrepreneurs landing in collaborative synthesizim to create massive local prosperity. Such advancement will impact thousands of cities and nations and will move towards faster advancements. Technocalamity is silently creating some 100 plus such mighty Micro Power Nations; their sum total of power will be far greater than any super power on the planet. Ignored and often abandoned they have now surfaced as a new combined force and new economic power.

FACT:
No single country is exclusive.
No single country has exclusivity to all mankind.
No single nation has all the virtues. No single nation has solutions.
for all the other nations.

The diversity of mankind is hardwired not to surrender to one single ideology or any one single culture or style.

Mankind is color-blind to race; deaf and mute to hate talk, open to all and demonstrate kindness to humanity. Mankind is also very resilient to adversity and strives for survival; the proof of its existence is not hidden in its stealth destructive capabilities, but rather centers on the constant nurturing of minds even under extreme tyranny and repression. The evolution of civilization, no matter how primitive in certain spots of the world is still the solid proof of this steady process.

How blatantly wrong are the so called brilliant and powerful people and nations of the day who are convinced that creating one single new world order under one control is the answer. This stupidity can be discovered in a simple common-sense journey and witnessing the real concept of creating one universal culture.

Modern day repression via fake news which exists under the strict rules of political correctness that eliminates intelligent debate and in turn lead to sound bites; they are the 'dog whistles' and divisive politics shredding the economic landscape.

Common sense issues… what if scenarios

America provides a land of millions of new opportunities.
India provides a land of millions of new entrepreneurs.
China provides a land of millions of amazing manufacturers.
Today's world is already filled with billion plus highly talented people.
When in time has there ever been such available talent?

Micro-Power-Nations are the new frontiers. It is time to create your own common-sense realities. Lee Iacocca, Chairman of the once mighty Chrysler automobile factory, said, "Lead, follow or get out of the way".

Why understanding incompetency is so critical?

The once mighty skilled hands for milking cows became useless on typewriters; pony express operations were replaced by automobile and office work was shifted to smart phones. Facing change is a lot of fun. Last year's high value functionalities are becoming new liabilities today. Face it, adjust and move on. Taking stands to resist will burry you in the avalanche. Technocalamity has isolated performances in fractional slices, where complex procedures are resolved instantly, making human interaction appear like chimps peeling bananas. It's cruel, it's reality, and it's hard. It is also very comforting when there is a gradual change and self-discovery all along the journey. We are now a rapidly advancing world and to live in a gradual change is critical. All over the world, the bureaucracy once considered as noble, with the offering of long-term job security, is now in meltdown. Fake agendas and hologramic economy followers were extremely successful in this fog. The two billion becoming unemployed in coming years are where all the prosperity issues are headed. The question is how to connect with intelligent dialogue, how to mobilize with pragmatism and how to create massive sustainable prosperity?

The Women Entrepreneurs

Within the last decade the number of women entrepreneurs has jumped to new heights worldwide. Driven by a new sense of freedom, technology to allow heavy lifting, what was impossible during the 'macho-men-only' era. Presently the political change where women were given respect and brought on frontline of national thought leadership. Every woman is already born an entrepreneur, just observe a mother how she dedicates the minimal resources and stretches to build a family with dedication and focus and ready to fight or give her life if necessary. Some 'macho-man-only-worlds' were often afraid of that power. No other factor raises high as the abuse and stripping of creative power from women in the households of the world, outside lip-service, no other policy neglected more as not freely allowing women at the true and real global entrepreneurial stage. Now the future is diverse, tolerant and gender free, technology the most powerful tool and provides global access for bold entrepreneurial women. Around the world with new awakening women are transforming and marching ahead. This will be a new frontier and requires advanced study.

The Real Fear: Wise and enlightened folks can clearly see the extreme beauty in chaos, where fluttering butterflies in the Amazonia can cause a cyclone thousands of miles away. We are all inter-connected and not understanding that full multi-directional points of connection, is the most dangerous deadly virus of humanity. It is way past time that we study global age challenges and fully realize that our diversity is what mandates our survival.

Glasshouse economies throwing stones are now living in shattered cathedrals but called nouveau architecture and recognized as victories.

Do not just read newspapers; also study the atlas very deeply.

Do not just pray; also study other religions with curiosity.

Do not hate; look at yourself daily in the mirror.

Do not just seek to destroy, show to build and create extreme value.

Do not just ask for, but also give generously.

Collaborative synthesizim

Why new global age is the dawn of a new Hundred Trillion-dollar global economy? This is when nouveau entrepreneurialism becomes intertwined with Technocalamity. It is driven by Alpha dreamers and creates a peaceful and very powerful collaborative synthesizim with the unique ability to dance altogether in right tempos and harmonious rhythms. Make the world great again. Collaborative Synthesizim is a new global age phenomenon that concentrates on new rethinking and relooking at the world, seeing it all over again, like never before, village by village, city by city; it requires that we re-explore the landscape of richness with new minds, visions of 2020 and beyond, with new sets of eyes, and with raw wild entrepreneurial imagination. Collaborative synthesizim is a highly integrated, technology based real time superior performance and collaborative progressions deployed simultaneously in dozens of countries with fascinating ease. It's global age rapid deployment of innovative excellence with new execution styles coming together to create massive impact. This is new thinking retrained, new visions reengineered and new business models recalibrated. It's a new blend of massive economic development that is synthesized at a new mix cycle rate, boldly declaring old economical thinking and business models ineffective. This is neither the fifth nor tenth industrial revolution; it's a brand-new renaissance of new global thinking

Finally, now, 20 billion smart devices in the hands of five billion Alpha dreamers will start dancing in synchronization at the same beat. This will be a real living tsunami of Technocalamity; it will be like being inside a big screen sci-fi film via goggles in your own privacy of space with your choice and time. The earth will vibrate with grassroots prosperity. Such a world will use primal mankind needs as a principal guide and overtake destructive maneuvering of self-interest-agendas. Alpha dreamers are like the new global age pioneers of today, liberating the old thought leaderships of yesterdays. The world is so big, so colorful and so wide open to massive collaboration; it has been the last century's dogmatic destruction, blindfolded by fake news, bad economic models and for-hire incompetent leaderships that have led to failure.

Entrepreneurialism is for entrepreneurs, like mountains peaks are for mountain climbers. The primary goals of entrepreneurialism are extreme value creation in a race toward commercialization, and extreme image generation in the face of global competitiveness all with boldness in pursuit of truth and large-scale problem solving. Around the world, absence of such open debates among various levels of national leadership and mandated agencies is clearly troublesome. Their lack of knowledge is tolerable; their lack of substance is understandable, but their lack of actions to advance the issues on understanding, deployment and mobilization for grassroots prosperity solutions are just not acceptable.

The fog of chaos: The popularity of entrepreneurialism like a branded umbrella for economic revival amongst top national leaderships of some 100 countries of the world has passed. The time for change is way past due. The deeper challenges of creating real actions must be addressed.

Fearing the billions of unemployed youth as a restless force are new challenges of today. Currently, all over the world, economical revivals of the middle class and grassroots prosperity struggle while burdened degree holders wonder aimlessly. However, in response, during the last decade all over the world, name-branded entrepreneurialism with recycled case studies on random innovative incubators and start-up programs activated but were unable to deliver shiny turnarounds. If innovation without commercialization is suffocation, incubation without entrepreneurialism is hallucination and searching for 'unicorns' is basically creating psychedelic economies. So, which way are we headed?

The Teleprompter Knowledge: Understanding of lip service and fake entrepreneurialism is essential. Ignoring the special knowledge of masses of existing small and medium enterprises sprinkled all over the nations already in the hands of experienced entrepreneurs, is a power national asset. This knowledge is ignored against hyper-trading, stock manipulations and fast buck globalization. Replaced and substituted by programs of entrepreneurial revival operated and managed by non-entrepreneurial is now a visible problem. Liberated use of the term 'entrepreneurs' does not create real entrepreneurialism.

On the topic of innovation and entrepreneurial projects, the current national leaderships are very fascinated with single day photo-ops or a single night of awards while nothing is delivered during the remaining 364 days of the year and void of real action. Today the public-private communities of the world have acquired the taste for innovation and start-ups, but they are still hungry and are demanding full course meals and possibly gourmet dinners. Memorizing a few books about smiley billionaires is not the best way to create entrepreneurialism. Just like chefs cannot pretend to be surgeons or firework assemblers as rocket scientists, entrepreneurialism is less about reading how one created a billion-dollar success stories. It is more about digging real trenches and self-discoveries. Classroom studies of books with millions of copies sold do not automatically create a Steve Jobs or Bill Gates. It might help a bit but it will not result in real economical turnarounds.

Fact: Classroom education is 'explicit knowledge' like bookkeeping, something that can be written. Entrepreneurialism is 'tacit knowledge' like riding a bike, something that can only be practiced.

Understanding Entrepreneurial Knowledge: All around the world, to create grassroots prosperity, the superiority of the message embedded in the art and science of entrepreneurialism is clearly written in the language and symbology of 'tacit knowledge'. This should not be the deterrent for the top business education academia for being so 'explicit-knowledge' dependent. It should not stop national leaders and their mandated agencies on economic growth for being so dependent on or subjected to academia.

This is the mega trap of entrepreneurial revival at major private-public projects on economic turnarounds. The obvious proof, around the world, is lack of real entrepreneurial talents at the very top. The lack of common sense and open dialogue are clearly an issue.

Methodologies: Uplifting entrepreneurial economies via entrepreneurial ways: Immersion: Create massive and total immersion of all programs already engaged on the entrepreneurial fronts in real time. Unlearning and evaluation are where active leadership acquire deep understanding and gets mandated to either lead follow or get out of the way.

Acknowledgements of Talents: Acknowledge entrepreneurial talents and contributions but let all the bureaucracy step aside. It is time to let all the fears, insecurities and lack of entrepreneurial experiences be kept apart and not become road blocks to already declared as stagnating factors.

Execution Styles: This approach is purely based on entrepreneurial models of execution and deployment. All simple common-sense approaches with mobilization that defies gravity is in direct opposition to bureaucratic and academic styles where holding back the intuitive uplifts of liberated entrepreneurialism suffocate growth and innovative excellence.

Mandatory Knowledge: Nestled in the traditional comfort zones of academic styles, tome of business plans and financial projections so badly prophesized as absolute necessity for any new venture leads to failure. Such demands would have easily killed the last 1000 game changing entrepreneurial revolutions. These game changers came out of pure and raw entrepreneurial thinking; they came from garages and mostly seat of the pants action plans. During the last half of this century the distinct rise of earth-shattering ventures and entrepreneurial genius is still not properly understood by academia or national administrative leadership. Let academia be academic this is where they shine, let entrepreneurs be entrepreneurs this is where they breathe. Combination is only possible when entrepreneurs start teaching academics, not the other way around.

Fact: The last 10,000 earth shattering global enterprises were created by entrepreneurs, most without any formal education or training on that particular industry. It's the entrepreneurial way.

Fact: Entrepreneurs openly admit their lack of knowledge against university trained professionals and still respect them as valuable technical experts to help them along their entrepreneurial journey. Why can't tenured professors teaching and writing books about entrepreneurialism with little or no knowledge of practiced entrepreneurialism do the same? Why are all the public entrepreneurial programs all over the world not being headed by solid and experienced entrepreneurs?

Fact: All over the world, suddenly, for the first time in a century, the term entrepreneurialism has surfaced as the most critically missing link of economic revival. The global mood now favorably swings from getting highly expensive degrees to being practicing entrepreneurialism as an essential talent. The search for better understanding and creation of fertile grounds for success has become a top political agenda item.

Fact: Where are the enemies; there are already millions of books on entrepreneurs and what entrepreneurship offers to the mankind, right from the Hunter Gatherers to modern day movers and shakers. There are also million case studies. What's missing is the critical analysis on who are the real enemies of entrepreneurialism and where are they hidden.

Fact: Why Entrepreneurialism is worshiped: despite being so feared and rejected at the early signs of out of box intuitions and the early incubation stages, but why is it passionately worshiped upon success? What's the cure for early rejection? What are the immediate and applicable pragmatic and measurable progressive plans that can be instantly applied?

The first person who simply demands a feasibility report or case study on the above before properly understanding and debating the subject is possibly one of the worst enemies of entrepreneurialism.

Raising the bar and asking difficult question:

What if there was a major national debate on entrepreneurial forces of a nation? Once again this is not about lip-service, plastic award night or churning academic case studies. This is bold and serious debates on how and where to incubate and where to deploy and strategize to mobilize. The superiority of the message demands real entrepreneurial practitioners in bold and raw discussions in collaborative formations. Nations have been singing songs of entrepreneurialism but without a full orchestra.

What if there was a national entrepreneurial manifesto? Once again, this is not about declaration of an entrepreneurial day, week or month where city halls, banks and parliaments hang banners and give commendation to failing incubators and startups. This is about solid understanding, respect and a clear game plan of deployment and mobilization.

What if there was a stage for entrepreneurs to express their issues and concerns? Once again this is not about large empty lobbies of small medium enterprise departments of the national administrations or long titles on fancy business cards. The obvious lack of knowledge and authority on these issues need creations of serious respectable permanent platforms hard core issues are discussed and pragmatic solution catered with promptness and care led by real practitioners. Nations have been offering invisible umbrellas of support but not where the real rain is falling. All over the world, the absence of special knowledge has now developed into living proof, that so far entrepreneurialism is a name branded lip service activity without real teeth. Unless this branded misnomer is purified with real and true entrepreneurialism it is simply one of the ghosts in the fog of the current chaos. Action is eminent.

How fast is the world advancing?

Recently, Alibaba sold USD$1 Billion in about a minute. This proves how technocalamity dances with global trade on the world stage. Cyclones of AI laced globally access digital platforms like LinkedIn and baby-Alibaba type models are coming like swarms. All around the world, such platforms will offer dramatically live interactive membership engagements and challenge the old traditional association formats. Now Chambers of Commerce and Trade Associations of the world are also being invited to global dance floors of greater prosperity. At such tradegroups level, this will require serious transformational turnaround to become savvy global age thinker and massively deploy their membership base towards global presence. This is not an easy task unless unlearning is the order. So how will this work?

Chapter Five

No Execution = No Innovation

National Mobilization of entrepreneurialism

Understanding national mobilization of entrepreneurialism protocols:

Many nations around the world have tried very hard to create entrepreneurialism but frequently failed. However, these same nations were able to create well trained armies and high-ranking officers because they were all trained in tactical battlefield engagements and by veterans from the real battlefields. Soldiers do not draw pictures of battlefields on whiteboards and run around with water pistols. They live the battles.

The above deployment and mobilization programs are primarily not funding dependent; they demand specific strategies and global age smartness. Most of the soft-infrastructure is already in place, and just need senior level workshops and deeper studies that must be critically mandated. With some 100 nations in the race, there are some 100,000 trade associations sprinkled all over the world showcasing their vertical trade sectors. Only a very small percentage, those with strong mandates to lead to prosperity for their members and showcase them to the world on a 24x7x365 basis with live engagement models are expected to change. There are ideas on blue prints, Cabinet Level guidance on deployments and 'national mobilization of entrepreneurialism' available on Google.

Classicism of Entrepreneurialism: The advanced study of classicism of entrepreneurialism brings us closer to global age mobilization and deployments of entrepreneurism as a new phenomenon. This new thinking advances mobilization of masses of entrepreneurs impacting grassroots prosperity captured by superpower new technology platforms. This philosophy challenges the current economic development models and raises the bar of entrepreneurial understanding. Entrepreneurialism is a national treasure and until these hidden talents are discovered and used, organizations and nations will be at a disadvantage. A nation's true and real asset if unexplored and unaccounted for as major and key economical values of underutilized natural resource, these talents and assets are wasted. Last century tabulations of economic activity measured sluggishly that gave the educated economist clout, where they pondered, forecasted and deployed academic theories. Today, live interactive smart and instant data challenges show flaws in old economical and hologramic models over the true entrepreneurial art of 'value creation' which is the prime concept of capitalism. The old fashion 'value manipulation' economy is faltering all over the world. New thinking is emerging.

What's stopping this? Why wouldn't a nation, already blessed with 1000 to 1,000,000 high value entrepreneurs mobilize and showcase them to the world, provide advanced global age skills and tools to grow and quadruple national exportability. It's not about armies landing on beaches to seek and destroy but about armies of entrepreneurs landing with collaborative synthesizim and innovative skills for mutual prosperity.

Silicon Valley was never forced upon postindustrial thinking of the corporate leadership of the day; it started out very quietly by smart techies toying in their garages creating their own hardware and software, tumbling into their own new terms and language with brand new voices and created a culture with extraordinary speed which needed to transform the world economies. It did transform the world; but this new global awakening with some billion entrepreneurs is 1000 times bigger now and it is still growing.

Why can't a national leadership make it a top priority to transform all trade bodies into super-digitized-global-performers for the global stage? What level of training would they themselves require to understand that such transformations do not require funding but rather on authoritative knowledge and global age execution?

The new entrepreneurial standards:

There are blueprints that lay out full deployment strategies. Once properly executed, such super innovative platforms encourage local political leaders, chambers of commerce, trade houses, major trade associations to join the charge, come altogether on the national stage and shine. This is a new global age way to mobilize entrepreneurialism and create a massive drive towards prosperity. Export and performance enhancement programs designed to quadruple innovative excellence and exportability are deployment ready multi-dimensional programs. Such deployments can transform a Nation's SME and midsize business owners seeking positive trajectory for outbound global growth.

Fact: The world can easily absorb unlimited exportable ideas in unlimited vertical markets.
Fact: The well-designed innovative ideas are worthy of such quadrupled volumes.
Fact: The entrepreneurial and dormant talents of a nation are capable of such tasks.
Fact: The new global age skills, knowledge and execution are now the missing links

The tools for such transformations are already available. Creating entrepreneurial prosperity is not that difficult but it demands high quality and high-speed smart execution that is compatible with entrepreneurial thinking and styles of operations. Why is this an attractive message? Potential political platforms and wake-up call for smart nations will create economic turnarounds?

Fact: We arrive soon at 2020 where new worldwide processes of block chained-economy starts eliminating some one billion white collar office workers. In the following 3650 days China becomes the world's largest economy, and the global shifts of image supremacy starts opening brand new doors. Where are those serious debates on mobilization of hidden talents?

Fact: Every night as we fall asleep, three quarter of the world is wide awake; churning, consuming, producing and dancing in its glory. The new hyper accelerated world is spinning without waiting for any one person or one mighty nation.

Selective nationalism

The Selective Nationalism: While civilization is diverse and mankind colorless and borderless, the current economies and the engines that feed mankind are often territorial and walled. Prosperity models demand territorial controls to measure inequalities, fair trade and national innovative excellence. Selective nationalism is increasingly in order; when nations set their own goals of creating grassroots prosperity and declare their citizens the number one choice recipient over other outsiders. When selective Nationalism challenges the current open globalism and demand juxtaposition of economic inequalities against creating grassroots prosperity, the citizenry enjoys continued progress. Nations are responding to the calls of their citizenry to manage their home base first.

Entrepreneurialization as remedy

Media is no longer the voice of the nation. The silent majority is the voice of the nation. The voice of liberty is truth; the purity of truth is when it's an open and an honest talk. Bulldozers of prosperity can arrive when Entrepreneurialization is deployed as a remedy: if properly deployed, as defined in The National Entrepreneurial Manifesto, it will create grassroots prosperity, and make economical victories impossible to stop. No other asset of a nation is more important or critical to the survival of a nation than the preservation of the talent of its citizenry; talents define the nation but need constant care and nurturing. It is the honest administration of hidden national talent and skill sets resources with strategic deployment that ensures successful results. Nations around the world can be easily differentiated on this matrix alone.

National entrepreneurial agenda

Entrepreneurial Manifesto is a prerequisite; in order to liberate entrepreneurialism within a nation on a grand scale but it requires a master blueprint to lay foundations as mandatory.

Fact: If entrepreneurialism is one of the most cherished traits that one could develops, it's also one of the most hated traits as others intentionally or unintentionally try very hard to crush. It's critically important to understand all aspects before undertaking a regional or a national program and make bold and corrective decisions, as this is beyond lip service and rhetoric delivered via Teleprompters.

Fact: Entrepreneurialism is not a measured or calibrated as a repeatable process. Each and every time, each single step is new and unique. That's why 10,000 case studies on Starbucks Coffee did not produce even one single player of identical stature. The pure and simple Fact is entrepreneurialism is orchestrated chaos in slow motion; a unique deployment of emotional intelligence with unpredictable sequences of actions striving for tangible and prosperous structure. There is no pill to instantly bring entrepreneurialism into action. There are methodologies that can create fertile grounds and ignite entrepreneurial thinking. But this is not explicit-knowledge that once understood and memorized there comes millions of accountants, doctors and engineers.

This is categorically different.

With a hundred plus countries in the race of innovative excellence and image supremacy of performance, few are scratching the surface of entrepreneurialism. Why? The deeper understanding required to mobilize massive numbers of 'job-seekers' to 'job creators' demands global knowledge, thinking and execution.

The new global age world is all about entrepreneurialism.

Fact: This decade the world will create far more new entrepreneurs than it ever did during its entire history. Never in history has so many options and free technologies collided with new ideas resulting with easy access to new ventures.

The chicken and egg debate on entrepreneurialism and its origin is almost out of place now. In the old days, often only the privileged had the luxury to try a new venture. This is no longer true; today anyone can start a business and if played correctly, can create direct access to billions, with very little or no cost.

Fact: The majority of the world's successful entrepreneurs never had formal education or training in the field they ventured into and yet they created monumental successes. There are stories after stories of great success global age entrepreneurs who were actually university drop outs.

It is also fair to say that entrepreneurs will freely talk about their failures. They look at failure as a temporary phase. Full trajectory of the glide path of any entrepreneur's life measures their own failures as a necessary part of the progressive journey. They learn to evaluate progress and correct very quickly. They plunged into an adventure and deployed highly specialized skills and experiences as they progressed to their goal.

A solid understanding is an absolute prerequisite.

Entrepreneurialism is not a course, a degree or a written methodology; it's all about understanding and experiences acquired by real living encounters; it's not 'explicit knowledge' like learning accounting, but rather 'tacit knowledge' like learning to swim or ride a bike. Entrepreneurialism is basically an event where all kinds of undefined and sometimes odd experiences of life are transformed into success. This success comes from preparation and when juxtaposed with the right opportunity, the entrepreneurial mind realizes that such chaos as opportunities and mobilizes a series of action, plans, and then gives birth to something dramatically out of the box. If higher business education primarily trained you to create a nice resume, demand an immediate refund because much bigger surprises are waiting.

The beauty of chaos

Risks are often pre-calculated and therefore pre-measured but opportunities are often open ended and, in the future, and therefore limitless and uncontrollable. Entrepreneurialism is rarely a calibrated trajectory towards mathematical equations or academic theories. Forget the old blueprints or cases studies. Entrepreneurialism is definitely original to its core; it is aggressively liberating from old routines and comfortable with 'let's rock the boat' vitality; it is a borderline revolutionary with progressive adjustments towards massive success. The academic mind, upon success, would probably call it a 'stroke of genius' where in reality it is 'innovative entrepreneurialism in action' referred to during incubation as 'out of the box' crazy and too risky thinking. The beauty of this chaos is in eye of an entrepreneur. Study how thousands of entrepreneurial ideas came out of chaos and distressed environments. None of that apparent confusion and chaos would be acceptable to the establishments of the period because it would be out of order and lack proof of financial success.

Failures are jigsaw pieces of winning and constant learning which will either score success or failures. This is an art that entrepreneurs are best at it. If they tumble, they only stand taller and ready themselves for the next venture. Turning big and small errors to support a bigger structure of success. Creating advantage, balancing chaos, looking at impossibilities as possible answers. They will immediately begin searching for the next round. They will stand up again and again until each and every part becomes and a natural part of the everyday processes. This is what an entrepreneur thinker does!

Entrepreneurialism phenomena further simplified.

As an example, in very broad strokes, a typical mother by nature is a great entrepreneur in action; observe how she takes limited resources, distributes them fairly, manages complex emotionally driven multiple tasks while continually nurturing and helping the family reach long term prosperity. Notice the balancing act, admire the intuitiveness to issues, and analyze the maternal instinct of protection. The focus becomes the needs of the family and her desire to guide the growth of the family. She is forever striving to help each member maximize potential. Admire her play on periodic chaos and equally see the responsive management of multiple methods needed to reach the outcomes from such situations. Appreciate, dealing with multiple sources of ignition, striving to win at all costs, while simultaneously dancing on several floors at different tempos, all with love and affection. Lastly and most importantly is her willingness to sacrifice anything and everything for the survival of her home and family. Every mother is a natural-born entrepreneur, but is often crushed by our culture, surroundings or men.

The cruelty of knowledge

Entrepreneurs are extremely knowledgeable in general and specially about their business models including innovative and weird 'stuff' as their super-creative 'thing'. They are real experts. They are masters of their discipline. After all, this so called undefined 'stuff' cannot be compared to any typical PhD program; nevertheless, deep down entrepreneurs are natural masters of their mysterious stuff, or the so called unknown, the unproven ideas of pre-discovery. Their knowledge on such weird notions or ideas, once commercialized successfully, is often more powerful than 1000 PhD packages of knowledge. Observe and you will quickly determine that these superstars are far superior to the 1000 University Deans or PhDs combined in their acquisition, utilization, and finalization of entrepreneurial ideas. Check out the top 10 entrepreneurs in any category anywhere in the world and you will see how their weird stuff was miles above other educated and well-trained experts and eventually resulted in something super special for our world.

Fact: Prime syllabi of any of the top MBA programs in the world today were once totally unknown subjects to universities; they were created and established by entrepreneurs of the time--from franchising, IT, e-commerce, social media, marketing, branding, customer relation, stock markets, mergers, and acquisition of knowledge. These were all later adopted by smart academicians and added into the MBA program and business curriculum.

The value of 'rocking the boat' is one of the most innovative and entrepreneurial maneuvers, and it is now being discovered by the academicians and historians as concepts of great value. Just watch a few movies on entrepreneurial heroes and discover how during their early years, before fame, they were considered monstrous trouble makers. This trouble making led to innovation and the pinnacle of entrepreneurship. Are you bold enough to assert yourself as an expert of at least ten times more knowledgeable than PhDs or best your boss's bosses by innovatively applying and using your own original ideas that shows sparks of the hidden 'stuff' that makes for an entrepreneur? You must prove your authoritative command here, or just be one of them.

Entrepreneurs never stop working. They love it and live it round the clock. The chaos centric entrepreneurism continues the march, leaving a cloud of dust for others to muddle through, bumping into each other and apologizing. This is how case studies get recorded in the dust clouds as entrepreneurial footprints.

Entrepreneurialism when raw is rarely visible in behavior; when refined it becomes noticeable in achievements; when perfected it becomes the new standard for others to create new theories and invent terminologies. Everything is a work in progress, all the time and every day new ideas are explored, added, evaluated and refined. Mistakes and errors are compiled as experiences and steps of advancements. Mistakes and errors are a total no-no situation for non-entrepreneurial. On the journey to higher academic achievements, entrepreneurs realize very early that rather than becoming an advanced scientist in genomes, they will create a company today and hire the best genome experts who are already equipped with their doctorates in the subject. This represents a saving of a decade of study and when multiplied by the additional assembly of other highly trained qualified talent's, become a saving of time equal to a life time.

Entrepreneurs venture on untraveled roads, enter dark tunnels and with no fear of possible train coming from the other side; they take chances, boldly and admit mistakes quickly, because they know that success is often hidden in mistakes. Consider this--around the world today, most of the highly qualified, educated, and certified individuals are working for an entrepreneur. No single organization of any kind or any size anywhere in the world would exist without the deployment powers of entrepreneurialism at the helm.

Are you happy about the way the world is going forward?

The mastery of failures

Learn fast, fail fast; learn fast, succeed fast. Most earth-shattering entrepreneurial projects around the world were in reality very long processes build on continuous slow and partial failures, wrapped with periodical successes and major break-throughs. Failure is a part of the entrepreneurial trajectory. Like going to a World Series games, where losing games along the journey is part of the game. Outsiders are always overly frightened of the failures and thus miss out on greater and hidden successes. Deeper study are the prerequisites. The mastery of failures teaches them on how to succeed.

The greatest misconception about entrepreneurialism, why they fail often. The answer they try often and win often. Why is failure considered so bad? No "World Series Games" of any kind, in any sport, would be at all possible if each competing team won each and every time. Some win and some lose, but both are champions. The failures add up and acquire extraordinary experiences and most valuable qualities towards the trajectory of success. The most powerful players have occasionally lost the most important games during the most critical times. None of those players were fired on the spot and unlike the corporate world, they were given extra support in order to overcome their defeats and use their losing experiences as critical bench marks. Why is the sporting world so different? Is it because the controlling industry has accepted the rules of winning as a process via managing losses? There is no team in the world that wins each and every game ever played. When will a national agenda start treating the journey of an entrepreneur as a game of winning, and at times losing, but in either case creating respect and appreciation for the number of games played? These teams are not punished or blocked for not scoring. They are considered well experienced.

Case Studies: Why burn the case studies? Why not, Case studies are not blue prints to success, they are traps created from the hearsay of others from past with little or no thought for the future. If creating a new business is simply based on other peoples' case studies it would be easy and could be taught via class room theories; if this was the case there would already be 10,000 companies like Apple, Google or Starbucks in the world.

Fact: Some USD100 million are wasted each year in buying dark color furniture and fancy espresso machines in support of crazy dreams like becoming another chain like Starbucks. The majority fail within first year. Why?

The case study dependency is the most flawed teaching doctrine; it is a safe play for novices. It is a serious fallacy to cover up lack of new knowledge and avoid any risk taking or out of the box innovative excellence while copycatting others with mediocrity. None of the original top star entrepreneurial businesses started out with a case study. To become a legend, originality and innovative excellence is the only path. Only feeble minds gravitate to copycatting. Discover the real and true depth of national entrepreneurial forces Identify experiences, certify global age skills, and reward warriors Declare immunity to entrepreneurial failures and acknowledge entrepreneurial perpetuity.

Create Cabinet Level debates and discussions to bring harmony to such critical debates

Global age; new realities new challenges

A Divided World: One half of the business world leaders are always winning as they are always playing by the rules – the other half of the business world leaders are always losing and not even aware that such rules exist. Open any old thick, glossy trade magazine and the proof of such ratios are right there. Just like a gemologist can better appreciate the cut of a diamond. A mastery of global age understanding is a prerequisite to deciphering the unfolding of a multi-faceted future. While on the other side, the age of abundance will continuously drown mediocrity and shred weaker business models. The constant overflow of great globally accessible and affordable ideas will crush parochial thinking and single-sided nationalism. The global-age culture will dominate and force reevaluation of everything. Superstar entrepreneurialism will be the most desired model.

All this combined has now created a new kind of cyclone on the horizon, something that the corporate nomenclature buzz and media pundits are still years away from finding the right 'name' for. The most skilled in global age entrepreneurialism and innovative excellence are trying to get realigned to face the new realities.

We are at the 3rd Decade of the 3rd Millennium. After the big fanfare at the end of year 2000, the first decade of the new millennium brought questionable wars. The second decade followed with national calamities and massive bailouts. This 3rd decade is poised to either bring down major economies or catapult them back into their glory days. Both are possible but require deeper understanding of the new landscape and new rules apply.

Reading future requires futuristic-literacy

How overflow of massive and almost free technology is now challenging our own skill gaps? How will the deployment of such mega forces bring prosperity and alter the local GDP? How will quadrupling exports achieve image supremacy of a nation? How will a master execution plan based on future timelines ensure success?

Geo-Entrepreneurial Transformation: new global ideologies for creative interdependencies. Examples of soft power asset management and innovative excellence: UBER is the world largest taxi service without owning a single vehicle. FACEBOOK is the largest social media without producing any of its own content. ALIBABA; is the world largest retailer without a single warehouse. AIRBNB is the biggest hotel provider without a single hotel. There are thousands of others similar examples scattered around the world.

The quality gaps and superior performance issues. Transformation from the 'schlocky' mentality of producing faster, cheaper, goods and services into a new global age thinking of becoming a new global age 'perfectionist' ideology of 'extreme value creation' fully supported in parallel with 'extreme image generation will become the new norm. If the world is overloaded with junk then producing more junk will not create new prosperity. Innovative and creative solutions, intertwined with quality and high branded vales will be a major change. If changes are not made ideas, both good and bad will simply die due to the lack of quality and the lack of global image positioning, but when both processes are deployed in parallel, image supremacy and innovative excellence success start to take shape. Currently swamped in the age of abundance, 'undervalued' goods and services are being offered in 'overvalued' and excessive packaging and have only brought the majority of businesses of today to their knees. The rules of engagement with the image supremacy protocols must be on the forefront for any survival.

Randomness of entrepreneurialism

If the entrepreneurial gene is widespread and massive job creation can only be solved by entrepreneurs, why is a nationwide program not a top priority of the country's national agenda? Let's face the harsh realities, governments all over the world became keenly interested in SMEs especially during last decade. Efforts, around the world have been initiated and the new global buzz of 'innovation, incubation and entrepreneurs' programs got priority. Now when the time comes to face the truth, can Mount Everest climbers be trained by librarians? What new measures will universities and other entrepreneurial programs have to deploy in order to ensure the quality of pure and natural entrepreneurial fertilization and execution? Is mass fertilization of superstar entrepreneurialism possible? Armies of entrepreneurs can be created just like creating MBA programs but this demands a mega shift in thinking, knowledge, and execution at the deep end of the organizational structures and academic corridors. When 'out of box 'thinking and 'risk taking' behaviors become a positive part of a national economic agenda major shifts will come. Entrepreneurialism will come when failure gets scored as a series of worthy experiences and not as a lost cause. When entrepreneurs under a national agenda are recognized as a part of a nation's assets. When the self-employed are given the same or more accreditation as any other professional. When risk-takers are showcased and not left in the backroom to be judged by other professionals. When job-creators get rewarded and not overtaxed with extra paper work as punishment. When entrepreneurs are asked to design major government programs on job-creation When non-job-creators are deemed less skillful in teaching entrepreneurialism by the book.

During the last century in America, difficult, unpredictable and unimaginable behavior and execution was considered as innovative excellence and applauded. Failures became part of the learning experiences as an asset and not a liability. Around the world, no other experiment of human endurance has been as successful as the story of the American people and their drive to free enterprise and entrepreneurialism. Now lost in an abstract economy, it still offers the best-trained and educated entrepreneurial citizenry and still provides the best trained minds and rapid-expansion national and global combinations compared to other nations. It's all about philosophy and game changing strategies.

Key points to memorize;

National mobilization of entrepreneurialism is the only logical way out for regions and nations already struggling for grassroots economic survival. Classroom training and incubation have failed, innovation without commercialization has failed, and small medium size businesses have been openly abandoned and teleprompter read promises has done nothing.

The world is wide open for good quality products and services and the only question is whether a nation blessed with good quality manufacturers and exports is capable to tango with a hundred plus countries. Otherwise their future gets increasingly darker. Local communities suffer.

Creating a national agenda to embrace all this as midsize economic turnaround is also a logical process. The demands are simple, re-group local trade associations, start on a new page of entrepreneurialism, exportability and innovative excellence on an organized basis for their entire memberships. Easy to say but this demands high speed execution and master game plans. Adding local Chambers of Commerce and local governments can add far more synthesizim.

The current economic chaos is a great opportunity to come out of the fog and face new realities and adopt advancing strategies for the wide-open world.

As university degrees have limited turnaround value, the entrepreneurial games have the bounce to leap frog ideas with innovation, incubation and start-ups, but all this requires coming together under one large umbrella of export centric mentality and tough scrutiny of quality control. For the last couple of decades, we got so used to fake hedge-funded economies, and artificial evaluations, that we lost touch with real value creation and real economy. To read the future we need to learn the future-language. Futuristic-literacy is the art and the science of value creation and is hidden in the entrepreneurial genes, combining all of the above creates an award-winning recipe but in need of master chefs.

Reality check, local prosperity

How many names of key people from businesses, trade-associations, chambers, government, federal, provincial, municipal, state, level plus universities and other selected organizations can you . How many of those are willing to assemble for a serious debate under one umbrella and engage in powerful but authoritative discussions with real options poised to seek immediate implementable ideas and strategies?

How to mobilize this style open thinking and how to pull up local hidden talents. How to stage and showcase their ideas and contribution to make them stars?

How to realize that such efforts and special programs are not funding dependent but rather demand execution and authoritative knowledge and global age solutions.

How to create a culture where entrepreneurialism is not feared. Often they are kept at close distance but not allowed to take a leadership role. How to create entrepreneurial economic turnaround which should also include diversity, tolerance and gender equality.

Chapter Six

Vision is not about seeing more, rather it is seeing less, but more clearly

Start living in future, starting today

Possibly by 2030: Top Ten Economies will have combined GDP of USD $200 trillion. To put in perspective, China and India will contribute $110 Trillion, USA $32 Trillion and Japan $7 Trillion. What does this mean to you, your mind, your mapping and journeys?

Deep study of micro-power-nations, new emerging economic giants, and their new game plans will provide very different blueprints over what the once established super-power nations are now leaving behind. The hardest part is to first understand and accept these massive global tectonic shifts and secondly to allow the mind to adjust to new rhythms. We must unlearn the past and relearn the future with highly special skills required for the new locally-national and globally-wide-open landscapes of 2020, 2030, 2040 and 2050. Every new decade will automatically demand additional quantum leaps of the mind, mental endurance, stamina and deployment skills which will decide any forward steps and progressions. Today, what's called knowledge, education or experience on complex and senior jobs is being replaced by new a mental capacity that only needs to figure out which right key to click, while properly reading ever-evolving landscapes are already drowning with unlimited free technologies.

The kind of work that keeps a billion executives overly-busy today will disappear into a single robotic click of tomorrow. This will leave billions of executives having to prove their newly acquired and upgraded mental capacity on such forefronts in order to remain of any value to any growing enterprises of the world. The new ultra-high demands based on mental-building are not body-building. Easily visible; like, splashing water on the beach or train like a Navy Seal, finger paint or design a smart-city or manage a single store or run global e-commerce for a giant global enterprise.

NONE of this will happen overnight;

Neither the global tectonic shifts nor your own self-discovery of the hidden deeper canyons or the greener valleys of your own mind will happen instantly. On that note, why is there panic today? Let's face it, those billion once mighty superpower executives are gasping to remain functional on their jobs today, not because there is a shortage of jobs, or work too complex, but because they lost the art and sciences of creating enterprise growth and grassroots prosperity.

Mediocrity has no room in this global age. Basically, innovation mantras failed without commercialization and this never happens without entrepreneurialism. That is why all over the world, decade-long campaigns on start-ups to create entrepreneurs and enterprises only created a very small and almost invisible impact. The world changed, while the processes, procedures and thinking remained the same. Understanding all of this is simple. The public sector learning upgrades are now far more obvious over private sector unlearning. The world of being busy and working hard with expensive repair-fixing equipment will not improve.

The global-age has now morphed the world; the metamorphosis has advanced, study very deeply but from a 'butterfly's vantage point' and not from a caterpillar's disposition. Allow your mind to travel as this is where your hidden mental powers transform into new ideas; spread wings and show colors while flying. The caterpillar's disposition only keeps one crawling.

Look around, city by city, at the developed economies, observe their trepidations, and notice their lack of skills now impacting their motivation. They are caught in a love and hate relationship with the new global age and their performance and output is becoming a liability to growth. They are no longer the real contributors that they were during the previous waves, decades ago.

While, at a snail's pace the world advanced and at the same snail's pace they blatantly abandoned thought, ignored global age thinking and failed to upgrades of new skills. Primarily, they were very comfortable with their timely education, prosperity and continued joy-riding the waves of the period. You can look at 2000 case studies and research the progression of commerce to learn about direct matches for skill developments. It might be more fruitful to ask for refunds for the MBA degrees where time was wasted on those case studies and skill matches. Global masses of graduates were convinced that these approaches to learning were for record-breaking lifetime prosperity. Today is no different. The lack of enterprise skills is where economic growth has collapsed. The internet and social media, over decades, provided serious distractions to learning, where the fake 'ups' and 'down' and useless 'likes' and 'dislikes' amused the already-stuck-minds of being super-successful. Decades of wars only created more fakery and dogmatism. Now unlearning and relearning in big and small, public and private organizations is the call of today.

Today, on internet intoxication and social media, Asia is already crazy about social media, but rather engaged as experienced and knowledgeable user. Certainly, not as much damaged as the West, where raw exposure over decades of experimentation now literally demands proof of mental capacity to demonstrate adequate and sufficient deciphering of facts and global age knowledge.

Fact: Information is power, but drowning in information is bad for mental health. Driving economic growth and prosperity agendas may demand mental endurance and performance road tests.

Across the world, however, only a minuscule percentage of enterprises and executives saw this and kept their upgrades and advanced with global age and today they already are in the top leadership positions and enjoying the arrival of the next waves.

Either you will have the brain-power to recognize this, emotional stamina ready to accept global shifts and mental endurance to start to unlearn and relearn processes to build yourself, or you simply allow yourself to work for some smart-robots with a leash just unpacked out of a box only for you. There are no other ways.

Unlearn the past and relearn the future
Unlearn to not only see with your eyes,
but also relearn to also see the same thing with your mind.
Unlearn to only hear the words in isolation
but relearn to hear also the hidden meanings

Tireless mind

If you get mentally tired, your own self-discovery will fix it. You can also fix it with100 books on Zen and meditation. There are references on anything to improve yourself, select, take action. Just adopt and apply

Tireless mind builds healthy bodies; there is no reason to be mentally tired Use the same books all over again
Boredom is a sign of being in a wrong place; change it
Creativity outbursts is a sign of bold advances; explore it
Anger is a sign of serious discomfort; eliminate it
Planning is a sign of understanding; improve it
Plan your hour, day, year and life; start all over again, and again, and again A smooth path will start to appear; try it out,
Keep planning; keep trying; keep planning, learn to plan to plan
The mind can do all that, very easily, and you just allow it to happen
Have a side talk with your mind, always
Stay in harmony, people, surroundings, nature and all
It's you and your smart mind exploring a journey of life; discover it

Survive or build, make a decision. Discover your own realities, challenges, task and carve your own future. If you are not a life-long learner, future will increasingly become darker. It's all about you and how you advance. The rest is all fakery.

The 360-Degree Frame of Mind

The main reason superb ideas and great people fail because they do not observe their challenges from all 360 degrees. The universe is not flat, it's three dimensional in perpetual motion. Everything in life is multidimensional and so is our thinking, as an example, if you see an apple or better an atlas globe only from the front, now imagine you never knew what was behind and now imagine your loss for not knowing half of your world. So, when you are baking, boiling or forging an idea but for some strange reason cannot see all 360 degrees you will miss the critical things. Like designing a bottle, but forgetting the bottom. The world of global innovation is riddled with millions of such mishaps, because only with extremely deeper and 360 degree looks and at times via accidental imagination ideas lingering for decades or centuries suddenly tumble upon discovering the missing bottoms or tops.

If you ever became a multidimensional thinker, something that normal culture and schooling never teaches you, you will need special training, meditation and Zen-like work to improve your thinking, something that demands to relearn and discovering what your mind is already so capable of doing. Retrain yourself to observe all your challenge and issues in various surroundings but in full circle frames of mind and now relearn to observe all things in a similar fashion, like your own little solar systems where object become suspended and simultaneously spinning in slow motion from all angles, thus answering with amazing options. This now advanced stage of thinking gives you commanding position to make quality decisions and speedy executions. What is 360 thinking when designing a wedding cake, electric car or a national political campaign. Splice your entire project on thinly sliced wafers and suspend them like a Carter Mobile. Study the discipline, genre, history and human interaction and keep thinking and tweaking continuously till the last day of the launch. Don't get shocked if the best ideas arrive on the last day. It is normal.

What you already call success or the First Success is in reality a gift given to you, based on where and what you were born with; from family, country, culture and surrounding, but your super success is what you discover on your own during your own journey and take off like a rocket, and here how fast you take action and deploy ideas gives you the differential edge. The future is about quality thinking, fast action, and only those societies with fast learning capabilities will out-shine others. Mankind has always survived and it has proven its resilience, despite the gloomy-doomy-talk, humans will improve their skills, they will match work and optimize machines to create more free time to become better thinkers and this will create better harmonious societies. Machines will eliminate human error. Better accounting, more transparency will eliminate cover-ups and corruption. This feature of Artificial Intelligence driven transparent accounting of national treasuries if properly applied will automatically quadruple global prosperity of the world. Today, the national employment numbers and GDP data are just old dead-beat data published to prolong economic incompetency that is sinking nations. Economic data and measurement rules need a mega change, that's why at WEF Davos no one dares to have a dedicated session on this.

Stupid data creating fake economy and political rhetoric, must be replaced with global-age transparent data to paint the honest picture. Economic punditry must surrender to these challenges. Having no time is no excuse.

Smart technologies will eventually liberate mankind

Mankind will have unlimited time available to become better thinkers

Mundane work done by technology will allow intellectual freedom

Better thinking and dialogue will create smarter growth and harmony

Honesty and integrity will prevail

Why are closely listening to new global age rhythms now mandatory? Old ears used to traditional public opinion polls and fakery are no longer valid. Therefore, every grassroots prosperity issue requires a mandatory process of self-discovery to first know exactly who you are, what is your understanding level followed by your own research on your favorite topics. Opinion polls and media is not the source. Without such processes of self-discovery to enable you to self-research on the topic on hand you might as well be just another spectator of the national brainwashed citizenry. Here your approval or rejection of this notion is completely irreverent, unless you can prove the clear differentiation of two distinct states of minds as enunciated here. Know who you are, demonstrate high quality thinking, articulate the topic with knowledge and authority listen with open mind and make intelligent discussions and create high level consensus.

Either you have enough credible knowledge and can objectively decipher and stand tall above nationalistic or dogmatic trash now a burden in global age or not. Simply, either you have brain power to cope and find solutions or remain radicalized with Social Media educated rhetoric to endless Babble. Those who have circumnavigated the world need no explanation here, those never touched other continents need very deep thinking to figure all this out.

Alpha dreamers are very comfortable in this space.

To build new ideas, you need your own enlightenment and global age thinking. Business success is basically a state of mind, highly agile and extremely responsible to its early deployment and mobilization. For example, Alibaba on day one was just a small obscure idea invented in the mind of Jack Ma, and from that moment forward, every single day in his daily mental frames this baby idea was consistently updated, invented and reinvented to its current stage with 600 million customers. The climb was gradual, but started out as a small brick parked in the mind of Jack Ma that later was transferred to his teams and to the world and now already built as one of the largest skyscrapers of the world. This is how Steve Job and million other thinkers, builders and earth-shaking deployment experts did. They build constantly, in their mind, where heart became the engine, body a temple of wisdom.

Three words, idea, crystallization and deployments, and the rest is history. Any successful enterprise is a manifestation and visual form of a vision crystalized. A vision is what creates and drives and later when fully developed, visible, touchable and executed it becomes a success story. Study top 100 entrepreneurs and their journeys to success, two things will amuse, firstly, that almost all had no special training of the business when the journey started, secondly, it was all upside-down ideas created in their own mind and unexplainable in any form in the early stages.

Two words, chaos and persistence. Entrepreneurialism thrives in chaos, now the entire world is in chaos and in sync with entrepreneurs, this out of the box and unusual global age combination is totally scary to non-entrepreneurial mentality. Never mind, as all depends on how much are you willing to change, how much are you are willing to self-explore and upon reaching a comfortable level of self-discovery and confidence how much are you going to deploy, and execute under what desires, goals and your own bigger agenda. It's all about you.

Once you have a vision, risk and fears components start disappearing. Remember, that door at the end of the hallway that no one was supposed to open, which petrified you all your life, and until you opened and discovered it was just a room full of junk. It was all about opening that door. Afterall, without self-discovery you will never see the room inside, just the door on the outside and wondering about inside. Without vision you will never acquire the search-light to peek in that dark room.

Remember the world's best teacher is You, helping and guiding yourself, and using your own mind to navigate and determine your own progress at your own comfortable speed. Exploring inner sanctums and wandering in your own cathedrals of knowledge and experiences, it automatically makes you the best guide on your self-discovery mission. You were born with all this in your head and subconscious.

Today, why you are your own best teacher, because the world has changed, universities are good if you wish to become a brain surgeon or proctologist, but to create an enterprise like Apple, Alibaba or Airbnb they may be your worst enemies. Learn the difference and march on your own, lead the charge.

Learn to understand "now" and enjoy living in the now moment. Study this well, as you master the art of living in the now moment you will acquire additional thinking to become a better time traveler into the future.

For advanced thinking start learning Living in Now moment as it is directly linked with Living in Future. Living at an ordinary level is like living in a regular pond, living at an advanced level is like living outside the pond and being fully aware of all surroundings, living in a now moment is being fully cognizant of how the things around you are being managed and this knowledge allows you to peek into your immediate future. This is all about awareness and understanding your surroundings and testing out your self-discovered talents.

Learning future; firstly, learn to live in the future, itemize your goals of today and how they tie-up with your potential achievements of tomorrow, secondly, learn to make prosperous future, itemize all things that are not working today and discover all possible substitutes.

Hard work is not future, smart work is.

You need advanced thinking and new occupational relearning, ignore the frightened old school's vantage point that only creates stand-still frozen state, turning minds into cement.

Are you a slave?

The Master of Robots will be smart unleaners,
The Slaves of Robots will be the deniers of change.

Three words, advance, advance and advance

Enterprise leadership has no clock; it's ready to be respond whenever and wherever needed. The fancy decorum, fanfare of the corner offices is for the bureaucratic title seekers. Real enterprise leaders are helpers and problem solvers. Typically, they are office-less and title-less as they are out there to make change happen. Drive the engines of human talent to create grassroots prosperity.

The future tools of the future are critically important; class room business education is an old tool-box, forget about it. Showcase your skills, internet-street-smartness, unlearning and relearning smartness, prove your multidimensional thinking and out of the box actions. The old and overly stretched calendar-based curricula slow education crawling that once fitted the agrarian era should stay in that era. This is the age of 24x7x365; world-class learning accessible from anywhere for almost free across the nation is the new model. Smart nations are aware of what is happening and they are exploring national deployment and mobilization of entrepreneurialism as the new frontier of economic turnarounds. Some 100 nations ready for national elections in 2019 will witness new restlessness amongst their citizenry.

In the coming years, Public Sector executives of the Western world may end up profusely apologizing to their national citizenry of blatantly failing and not opening windows to allow winds of change to flow during the last decades. Their hard-cemented bureaucracies fermented their levels of in-competencies now directly related to repeated failures on national economic performance. On the same note the national academia may also finally accept to surrender at least on business and entrepreneurial educational fronts, write-off a trillion dollar in student-loans and ask forgiveness from the billions struggling graduates. The damage is openly visible.

Knowledge plugs and being wired to a new global universe will eliminate the B schools' MBA monopoly.

The journey of self-discovery will give you a start of a solid foundation, because without that, your very deep and very unique curiosity will never get awakened, you would be left like just another spectator. Know yourself deeply, know your craft and tie that with your special goals but all in perfect harmony.

This process will show you paths, you and only you, will only know your desired direction, your comfort and confident level will make you fearless and ready to face the head winds, as you move forward you will have all this figured out. Remember, it's you and all these issues that are between yourself and your mind. The discovery of answers to your quest will match your stamina, attitudes and your goals fitting to your special surroundings. You will feel good and very positive towards your challenges. You will know when it's working. Others will start noticing change in you.

Study deeply and challenge yourself on the big problems you have right in front; check from every angle, start all over, again and again. Consistency, persistence and acquiring mastery is where the answers are hidden. Soon you will learn that how desires and goals make you tireless, others will start praising your stamina.

You will know very soon, as you advance that how unique you are and why you always have better appreciation and understanding of issues on the table. Without a business card, title or corner office, you will come out as a leader and all due to your command and skills on the subject. All this exploring will feel like a natural process. From this point forward, you will demonstrate your focus and build your idea brick by brick and others will be in awe. You will become unstoppable.

Why you? Because you can think as your self-discovery allows you, your skills and craftsmanship are what your mastery allows you and your progression is what your curiosity has shown you and your solutions is what your mind allows you. All this becomes your natural path

Everyone will have all kinds of suggestions and ideas for you, good or bad, and everyone would like you to avoid mistakes on your journey, all these folks though very naive about your dreams may just simply be, trying to help you. Be extremely careful here, as you may get derailed. They will never have your depth, they will never understand your logical sequencing or your models, they will never have your guts, so ignore them. You, your mind and your goals are the drivers, if you have to please everyone, become a PR expert and work for an agency. Study the top builders and witness the chaos created by their closest family, friends and advisor. You just improve as you go along, no matter how long the journey. It will all work out.

You will also understand the notion why out there, success to so many is directly related to making billions. Why the general notion of building something is so stupidly related to how much money you make, right away. You will also know that the world doesn't understand why you are so focused on solving some critical problem, why so locally, nationally or so globally focused, they will never understand why you are so driven seeking solutions and not chasing a money-making scheme. Because as a builder you are on a very different path. The world needs solutions, the world respects solution providers and rewards them very well, but only upon success otherwise the world ignores you. Leadership with a clear vision is often a very lonely place. Others without vision and clarity and social media hungry dependency are blinded on such notions of building great ideas with extreme care and performance. People who get depressed because they got less 'likes' on their media post are neither your advisors or supporters, because their mind is not controlled by them, but by sophisticated algorithms. You will know all this very well. You hold a double edge sword. At times hanging over your head. This will also never bother you because your self-discovery, self-optimization and your heart and mind have all teamed up, to march forward. March ahead, leave a dust trail for historians to capture your journey.

Out there is a super competitive world, only the very best survive, call it whatever, ideas clicking with hard work and some risk-taking combinations to become legends. Mastery of multiple disciplines and self-discovery will draw your blueprints to navigate, your own tempo to advance and most importantly your own faith in your goals and realization that nobody in the world cares why you are doing all this. A new world waits for you, but only upon completion, this is when your performance is fully delivered and your concept successfully proven. Now they will all start chasing you. Observe how often they will claim that all along in their heart they knew right from the beginning about your pending success. Just smile.

To entrepreneurs and deliverers of new workable ideas it's not just a money chase rather a solving problem-solving chase.

Discover your 'on' and 'off' switch, how and when you are ready to go in action anytime, for example, every morning, you do not require a pack of cigarettes, liter of coffee and pep-talks, because you are a soldier in the battle all the time. When off, you close your eyes and dive in a sleep, you do not require bottles of tranquilizers and lullabies to go to sleep. Study 100 entrepreneurs and observe they have an 'on' and 'off' switches. Thy control their body and mind to achieve very superior performance. All the time, and whenever required. Instant action.

Discover your own questions, find them, add them, answer them, learn via this process, train yourself to become an organized thinker, thinking without organizational structure is simply drifting. Drifting is good, but find the difference between organized thinking and wondering without compass. Both are good, both have values but for builders of ideas, organized thinking is critical.

All of the above will make you a magnet, your talent will attract other talent, your ideas combined with talent and delivery will attract funding for growth and all this will lead to success and continuity.

Remember majority fail in these steps because they are deemed weak, in conviction; depth, originality, creativity, details, styles, personality, talent

85

management, execution and dozens of others from habits and integrity to family life issues. Once you have mastered self-discovery and your mastery of your own craft you will find answers to such challenges and adjust fast, fail but still adjust fast, problems but still fix much faster. You will know your weaknesses and fill them by attracting the missing talents.

Observe the true builders, they make more mistakes than average, but their success rate is higher. They accept mistake faster and correct them even faster, they also learn quickly to not repeat same errors. They are humans but on a mission. For every marathon runner there are thousands of spectators. They are just driven to get to the post.

You must learn soon if you are a marathon runner
Carve your own path, run at your speed and win

Alpha dreamers have two choices,

Just survive or build; build anything from anything small to an empire…

Two simple options, it's your choice, both options are available and easily manageable. Firstly, it's all about selecting a course of action and secondly, it is about finding the right methodologies. When building anything, be it a well-toned healthy body or becoming a maestro or virtuoso in anything, be it the arts, sciences or business, it's all about invested hours and how to feed the uncontrollable passion and desires. It is all about setting goals and reaching those goals. Once the goals are established, passion added, plan established, all the rest becomes simple.

There are already immense references available on how to survive, manage smooth or difficult times, cope with financial battles, survive socio-economic issues, survive personal growth aspects, and deal with varying life styles. We have coped with big, small and part-time jobs; we have planned hobbies and handled personal desires and adjusted odd habits. However, there is a critical shortage of information on how to create ideas and strategies for new growth. There is difficulty to turn for help in determining what shapes growth might take as builders differentiate possible styles, design and structural forms. There are obstacles in finding references for builders as they transform insignificant ideas into earth shattering mega realities.

Builders of ideas, all over the world have clearly stood out as lone warriors, creating major impacts on our lives. They are out of the ordinary but fearless in pursuit of their goals. They simply create life-altering small enterprises to massive global empires. The question becomes how do they alter reality and transform their thinking in order to reach for the unknown?

They all had one thing in common; they passionately choose building something and openly rejected just surviving. The majority of builders had ordinary lives and at times had difficult early years. Somehow, they discovered themselves at an early age; they knew their direction and became passionate about their specific interests and relentless in its pursuit. At the time they were not as much concerned about success or failure.

They were un-concerned of rejection by others, friends or families. They were tireless in their efforts, ageless in their thinking and fearless of external factors. They just kept marching ahead towards their goal, building each part of the goal stone by stone.

Marriott did not build millions of rooms for him to live in, and neither did Ray Kroc flip billions of hamburgers to eat himself. Such dreamers were simply driven to make something original. They realized what society needed, dreamed big to create change, and wanted to make life easy and help societies. This of course created immense wealth for themselves, which they accepted. However, that never made major changing in their original habits and lifestyles as they built new concepts and ideas. Money making was not their prime goal to begin with. Money and profits were simply accepted as by-products of their successful journey. If money-making had been their sole purpose, they would never have taken the risks necessary to build and would have gone into some quick money-making schemes.

The bottom line is anyone can build. Mankind is simply hardwired to succeed; otherwise we would still be in caves. Here is a critical yet simple step by step analysis and pragmatic methodologies that creates and defines builders.

What did Tesla see in the electricity spark, or what did Disney see in a field mouse, or what did Job see in computerized communications? It is all about curiosity. We are all born curious. Just observe a baby for a few minutes. When curiosity links to our traits, personality and temperament it opens amazing doors. More advanced thinking kicks in. Somewhere in these unique and personal processes, surrounded in our immediate surroundings and our external stimuli, all this works, and the results in some mysterious synchronization. Here, suddenly the day dreaming of lingering days turn into serious decision-making-tools to firmly adopt lifelong goals and commitments to become a builder of ideas and new things. Builders live a happy simple life; they just place building a top priority over everything including just living or surviving. This is where new ideas start to flourish and this is where small fires in pursuit of becoming a mega-builder are kindled.

If we compressed our last two thousand years of civilization into two minutes, we are right now only cognizant of the builders and innovators of the last fifteen seconds. We have no idea who came up with a saw, a hammer or a ladder during the first minute. Irrespective, during the last two minutes of our compressed history, builders created most of modern civilization. However, in any event and in the final analysis, it's always a personal choice or whether to build or just survive.

In choosing to become a creator of new ideas and build something of value, there is no duress; there is no force or organizational body that suppresses. It involves some serious free-flowing ideas attracted to your inner forces, will power, courage and bold commitments. It demands extraordinary focus and work toward the goals in order to assure advancement and to make small ideas grow into grand realities. The process is simple. This stage of choosing and discovering internal and instinctive talents is always a natural call. It is purely effortless, kindling raw imagination as this stage is very magical. It is filled with rainbows, twilights, sun shines and moon glows and is like falling in love at first sight.

Chapter Seven

Dream all the time, but execute every second

Builders are dreamers...dreamers are builders...

Building happens when sleeping talents and traits collide with their new and strange surroundings and result in creating fireworks. Combinations of oddities, chaos and confusion are often credited to entrepreneurs as such hectic process to them is just a normal slow-motion day.

At the same time, such processes of madly falling in love about an idea at the starting gates, often makes no-sense. At this point there is no justification, no financial rational, no business or boardroom protocols. Historians have already recorded such deep emotional moments of early chaos on thousands of the world's greatest idea builders. Frequently it seems that they simply tumbled upon an idea and then commit their entire lives to its creation. The world screamed and rejected their pursuits and labeled the creators as crazy. In printed and recorded history, the world is full of comments on how great successful ideas were originally written up on a handkerchief or a serviette. Once these creative ideas were built, their creators became legends and became stuff for universities to develop case-studies about and the builders were immortalized in books and statues made to honor their goals.

You will never know your own hidden super success unless you revisit your struggles and failures and discover the gems of experiences.

Be nice to pigeons who knows one day they may make a statue of you

Let's go deeper; let's explore to see if you are already a builder and then discover what can make you a legend. Building is more about discovering our hidden capabilities and polishing them in such a way that the processes of testing and advancements becomes a very enjoyable trajectory filled with new ideas, connecting with new shapes, molds and amazing processes, and then turning them into larger than life themes and structures. These are the makings of an enterprise. All this thinking and working leads to prosperity; the paths are straight, winding or extremely rough, but whatever the shape it's all about self-discovery and mental stamina on how to go about such long journeys.

Our birthright curiosity desires to learn and advance. Our leadership skills want to grow ahead of our surroundings. These are our free gifts often kept in safekeeping and NOT readily available for use. Often, we keep them wrapped and tucked away. They will work for us only if we play with them and allow them to bounce freely with our deeper and hidden talents. They will work for us when we optimize them. They will work within our surrounding no matter how difficult or cumbersome these surroundings may be. Self-discovery is a must. There may be hidden passages that will enable us to discover a magical blueprint of an idea or something to build and bring to fruition. The world of five billion inter-connected via multiple devices and Internet, are just waiting for new ideas. This world of commerce, where all is filled with noises, chaos and the screams, is clambering in this bedlam; the noises are for creating productivity; the chaos around creating performance and the screams to achieve some profitability are loud and clear. Without productivity, performance and profitability building, commercialization will have no purpose, value or meaning. Although, these notions are very well understood all over the world, in reality they are considered almost impossible hurdles to overcome. How can the impossible thinking be fixed?

What are the simple and pragmatic solutions? Typically, when there is an amazing idea, one can apply three styles of ideas-building-strategies; build it as if you were building a single dwelling, or you can approach it as if you are planning a landmark skyscraper.

This analogy has nothing to do with actual construction, but this type of thinking allows the mind to glide though the architectural stages and balanced requirements of deployment of raw materials as easily understood mental and logical processes.

Some ideas are like building a single dwelling: any person, any age, anywhere, can build anything. An idea normally is a shiny spark in the mental cathedral and you as the beholder of that beauty can see that spark and visualize how it can be turned into just a flame or a huge bonfire. Your talents can easily determine this. The different stages it takes to transform from a spark into a huge reality takes extraordinary combinations of skills. And the good news is that these are very often already hidden behind our normally accepted public façade. They are in your safekeeping for you and ready for use. Sometimes your hidden skills automatically respond to your sparks and kindle new bonfires; this is when intuitive and hidden talents naturally come to the surface.

Self-discovery is the secret to creating a life-long purpose and meaningful trajectory. The human body and mind are already capable of extraordinary skills; the world greatest artists, writers, scientists, politicians, astronauts, actors, singers and owners of the world's largest businesses had no ideas where they would end in their life while passing through their early years. Their sparks came in their own mysterious way; these creative thinkers just unfolded and discovered their hidden talents; they just vigorously kept polishing their inner crafts and kept the pace of hard effort and offered whatever their trajectory called for. This is a solid proof that we all have talents. Our potential is huge. It is something we possess and most of us know nothing about how to bring that potential forward. When we discover it miracles happen? Some of us discover it and then ignore it because it is too demanding. Success is already a tough road and super success is a very competitive trajectory. It's always the talents we apply that make the goals effortless. It is the steady planning and constant self-discovery that makes for the progress a smooth journey.

When closely reviewing the process of building an idea it's similar to building a single dwelling home. No matter what size, types or styles of big or small structures, the process of building and advancements are all synchronized efforts with great similarities. All good ideas need a solid foundation that gradually and beautifully shapes into adopting pragmatic structures around it. This style of architectural thinking creates a balanced progress, and can help shape an idea with solid structure.

An idea is like a flame like a kindle becoming a bonfire or a pebble on the beach waiting for the next tsunami, and they are always in desperate need of clarity and structures in order to mold them into the shape that will transform into reality. This is how a battery transforms into an electric car, a fan into a drone, and air-mattresses into Airbnb. The objective behind this imaginary process of porting an idea from the brain into reality is like creating a house. We can deliver something unique and of long-lasting value when we use our potential to provide mental blueprints and schematics that give shape to a sparkling idea. We just add some logical timelines and not allow it to just fade away in your thought stream. So now the idea needs a solid foundation; it needs a series of walls, compartments for different issues, a roof as master guide and all the other parts to make it livable. When an idea is presented in such detail and character it starts taking a successful shape.

10 Building Materials

These are critically essential to build great new ideas, deployments and mobilization on grand scale? Reading this book will NOT automatically make you a super builder of ideas, but it will open new windows in your mind. It will provide blueprints on innovative thinking styles.

Doing some practical and actual applications will also not give you mastery, but it will show you what can be achieved. It will also expose some of your hidden and unknown talents. Practicing this thinking and exe-cution of it will not change your life, but it will prove your determination to try and also take a plunge.

Change is in your head, already waiting for new instructions, if you only uncap and recognize your own strengths and commit to developing to new height and spending time on thinking and executing while meticu-lously monitoring your progress and making refinements for as long as it takes.

You have to become a real professional player and with practice you will acquire mastery of some of the goals, key skills, and related items. Basi-cally, you drive the car to become a professional race car driver. The car by itself will not drive you anywhere, you do the actual driving. This is all about you. This is about long-term game plans with better vision, execution and stamina.

A lot has been discussed here, but each item is like a tree with branches of its own knowledge, and you must be willing to select and create a new garden and plant the tress in different patterns to fit your needs of shades and esthetics. However, without daily nurturing and care noth-ing will happen. The blossom is all about watering and care. This is all about transformation; this is about new thinking and this about creat-ing massive growth. These may be tedious tasks that require focus and determination and steady course to arrive at success. This is not easy. Because this is not a glib motivational talk; this is very hard-core sub-stance, much like digging trenches in the middle of hailstorms. Study, decide and act on your own-self-discovery. Your own self-optimization and your own level of desired mastery. Success is a wide-open path.

The following sections are like blueprints and if it requires opening up big windows on the walls, you can select hundreds of designs and hun-dreds of techniques to install them. For every line and for every page there are unlimited possibilities available. Once you select your paths, strategies can carve out your own detailed and customized blueprints to fit your personality, capacity, stamina and your willingness to put the required hours into reaching real goals.

You must be cognizant of the Fact that there are over a million consultants almost freely available on the Internet and millions of new books of shapes and sizes are easily available, each claiming miraculous turnarounds. You can only select and deal with a miniscule portion of this abundance of knowledge and massive clutter. Clutter is the enemy of focus and unnecessary humming and buzzing brains that create fog are enemies of decision making. Frequently this abundance of free-flow ideas are worst enemies that must be unlearned and your brain uncluttered so your deep mind can explore new concepts and ideas. This is especially true as you progress with full awareness where you can use your new thinking as hidden tools to climb to the top of the pyramid. Equally, it's important to know that once you have decided on your master plan, for example, one of the key aspects of refinement may be a call for a selected color. When you arrive at such a progressive state, the choices of colors suddenly become freely available, with hundreds of references on how to use color. Refinement and progression are critical to select and search the most needed components, whether you are searching for new types of business models or styles from fashion clothing to creating series for telemovies or selecting global corporate identity, it's all out there. However, this almost free unlimited massive knowledge clustered like a mega city garbage dump only becomes valuable after a well refined and shinning pyramid of knowledge is structured in your head first and later gets ready for execution. This will protect you from drowning in massive heaps and dumps of knowledge. This is how you will create the differentiation between a novice and a global icon. Focused on the top-level structures and the critical steps needed for a special steady climb to delivering unbelievable ideas and configurations to claim the spotlight. As out there most is information-overload-anxiety and super-confused-social-media-punditry.

Take this as an exercise, imagine this like a blueprint of something, like a blueprint of a house and if it calls to setting up the windows on the walls, now you can select hundreds of designs and hundreds of techniques to install all kinds of windows and designs. For every line on every page of your blueprint there are unlimited references available out there. Your talent and wisdom will guide you. Once you select your paths and strategies you can carve your own detailed and create customized blueprints to fit your personality, capacity, stamina and your willingness to put the required hours to get to your real goals. Imagine your new ideas like building custom design homes and the usage global research to design it wall by wall, window by window, provides the logical methodology.

Knowledge is stacked like a shape of a pyramid that takes you to the top of enlightenment and, it's critical to understand how to avoid clutter of knowledge and only work with structural ideas that will organize your mind like a well-balanced and pointed design and structure not just a large heap of garbage in a dump.

You must be cognizant of the Fact that with millions of consultants almost freely available on the internet and millions of new books of all shapes and sizes claiming miraculous turnaround, you can only select and deal with a miniscule portion of this abundance of knowledge and massive clutter. Clutter is the enemy of focus with its humming and buzzing brains creating fog and getting in the way of decision making. The abundance of free-flow ideas are enemies unless we unlearn, relearn and un-clutter our minds, especially now as you progress with full awareness. You can use this new thinking as hidden tools to climb to the pyramid of prosperity. Equally, it's important to know how you can expand this thinking. For example once you have decided on your master idea to build and once the plan is refined to the point that you need a color, then there are already, feely available, hundreds of references on the use of color types to styles from clothing to corporate identity...it's all out there but it is only valuable when a shining pyramid of knowledge seeks for it, versus drowning in a massive heap of knowledge. This book is fundamentally focused on the top-level structures for a special steady climb.

The Mantras

I think and I can, I think and I can, I think and I can

For any heavy-lifting from your own self-discovery to self-optimization to superior performance you need three things, thinking, thinking and thinking... as it's all about your mind and how you use it to think in an organized fashion. Nothing else is more important

Building and execution within your surroundings needs three things, practice, practice and practice... as it's all about how you repeatedly use your mental skills. Without practice you are novice

Performance and endurance require three things, rest, rest, and rest... it's all about mental calmness to slow down your mind to relax. Without shutting noises in your head, you are stuck where you started from.

Mastering the craft and becoming a relaxed champion requires three things, learning, unlearning and relearning...it's all about intertwined transformational change. Without this you are only sliding back.

The mantra is all about making your mind a friend and creating new working alliances within yourself.

Well trained minds are capable to simultaneously creating innovative ideas and then confidently executing those ideas with clear and calm decision making. This can only be achieved with practice and by bringing new learning to the forefront. Invent your own mantras.

If you know the real power of your mind and can harness just a minuscule portion of it, you will become many times more productive. You will be many times smarter. As you become more familiar all this refinement will become second nature.

Remember, in this global age, if you rely only on your hard work and education, you may simply be left behind. Why?

Today, hard work has little value; smart work leads to success.

Today, University learning has less value; it is Internet-street-smartness, entrepreneurial smartness, global age smartness and all such combined will that lead to progress.

To become part of the Top 1% wealth club is not easy. Either you are born into this club or get pulled into it via spousal or educational arrangement. Rest is just grinding on the other side of the railway tracks.

The other option is to build something of amazing value that will catapult you into that 1% percentile club

So, either you build or just survive; either way, it's always your option, your choice and your performance.

Complaining about other people's wealth and about equality is pure nonsense. It is time to wake up and prove yourself.

Alpha dreamers have openness of mind because their expanded knowledge sources are much more than just newspapers, magazines, television and class room education; today, each and every one, singularly or collectively holds a powerful universal 'knowledge-plug' the internet. The internet's knowledge is delivered to their palm in the form of smart phone and other devices that virtually connect Alpha dreamers to the world. They are now increasingly developing common sense skills to decipher between truth and fakery.

Alpha dreamers are now smarter than any other group ever assembled in our civilization. They can dream a better future for mankind. They have been exposed to technology-infused-culture, technology-laced-reasoning and technology-manipulated fakery. Now they can operate their own free information-blenders at their own speed. The local, national and global hierarchies and dysfunctional structures are now more easily and clearly visible to them. This is now an unstoppable force chasing survival strategies. A new threshold for prosperity building ideas for the mankind is easily available and ready for use.

Top ten building materials

Ideas without structure and execution details have little or no value.

Ideas that demand massive structuring and Ground Flooring; why these foundations are needed for more interesting and complex ideas? Here a person can build an organization of any size or any type anywhere in the world. Such development requires understanding of the ground floor. How important is a ground floor in creating a tall structure? The size, space, height of a building is based on the structure of the ground floor. The ground floor determines how subsequent floors are added and establish the full functionalities of that structure. An architect diligently studies for years to acquire such skills and knowledge; the entrepreneur architect of an enterprise also has the same prerequisites. Therefore, no matter how simple or complex, the ground flooring demands meticulous planning and structuring. This analogy of building a multistory structure means that we keep the end product in mind and constantly visualize that product as we progressively advance.

Ideas Seeking Skyscapering: when a person wants to create a super idea or a superior global age organization, we must see the structure as a shiny skyscraper visible on the city skyline. This analogy meticulously outlines the step by step processes required to reach greatness. The rules of engagement require the three-dimensional applications of cement and steel structuring, balancing the arches and spans, and complete understanding of how to shape something grand and very iconic.

Chapter Eight

To experience tomorrow better, learn to live in day after tomorrow

Strategy One: Technocalamity

Definition: When the overflow of free technology drowns old establishments and allows new young ones to become iconic leaders.

Usage: to build any new idea demands solid understanding of technology that can be used throughout the concepts with an architectural sense of structure and balance in order to allow technological hold on all functions from top to bottom of the enterprise.

Symptoms: Long innovative process are now failing on commercialization; things have moved into unknown; new thinking is required; skill gaps are visible; finger pointing and panicky cost-cutting is the new rule. New technologies are drowning old thinking. What is next?

Can you erect a skyscraper without steel and cement?

Following are the ten key ingredients that are required to build brilliantly from the master design and blueprints, to the products of steel and cement, to the functioning of elevators, floor tiles and glass windows in order to produce a splendid structure. Each and every component becomes important because they are all the ingredients that eventually shape the structure into a smooth and beautiful design that moves from vision to a superbly structured structure. This is how ideas are put into action.

Should we avoid deep diving into freely available technologies?

Idea-Structuring and how to use Technocalamity in your planning: designing architecturally sound idea structures based on current overflow of almost free technologies, how to apply as builder?

Fact: ...when the tsunami of free technologies makes already established organizations look increasingly outdated, while the newcomers, the same tsunamis can quadruple exports, innovative excellence and catapult organizations into achieving image supremacy...this makes Technocalamity, the new global age phenomenon...

Every touchpoint between internal and external contact, whether prospect or customer, supplier or other must have a digital foot-print, captured and harnessed on specific timelines to make a super connected grid as part of the organization. Every member of the organization must spend some fixed time daily to understand where the flow of technology is headed, how its nature being 'alive' impacts the organization, and why it is moving in those particular directions may become extremely advantageous. To become a fully digitalized organization, once mind accepts it all this becomes easy. The majority of these efforts are almost free; all the heavy work is in internal adjustments and having the will to make a serious digital change and to adjust mentally and physically. Embrace technology at each and every step of the enterprise

Every big or small new idea is hungry for formal structure so it can come out of the fog, face reality, face global age competition and demonstrate clarity. Therefore, every idea needs to be initially tested in the mind. We must see clearly how it will grow and become a solid structure. This is critical at the early stage because right out of the gates, we must determine the shape of the idea. It is like stepping out of showers on wet floors or when missing green lights on roads, if we are not careful, ideas slip and slide within our mind at free-flow speeds and we can lose sub-stance. It's only the logical sequencing that make the ideas start showing permanence, start growing, taking shape, and move toward super iconic structures. It's all about how ideas are eventually structured in the mind way before they move into reality.

Today, ideas must deal with technologies. A century ago electricity played a key role in structuring or expanding the reach of an idea. Without a deep understanding on how technology works, we will be lost. Technol-ogy is the flying carpet that makes ideas grow; it is a serious challenge. In most cases it does not requires a degree in IT, but rather an open mind that allows technology to become an active tool. Technocalamity is where there are overflows of free technologies available for use. This new tool is drowning old established organization and at the same time it is creating massive new players with smarter ideas. This study provides the structural depth needed today; it's all about technology. Without a technologically driven structure, whether a political campaign, block-chain, franchise, e-commerce or a global age enterprise, the structure will simply not grow or survive without the use of these advanced tools.

How to create a sound structure to go upward and hold against storms and hurricanes? It is like designing and building with architecturally sound structures based on untapped and almost free technologies. It is all about utilizing the smart and intelligent systems and knowledge of the new global age.

How to apply all these amazing ideas as a builder:

Think digital from the start. Use virtualization as a base. It is like put-ting on special glasses and seeing the world in moving actions...this is where global age thinking and follow through are headed. You must not ignore this as a builder of new ideas. Every point from beginning to end, from idea to a finished product or service, from internal and external leads to billion points of contacts from customers to supplier and oth-ers but all with digital footprints. Each footprint must be captured and harnessed on timelines to make a super connected organization. This is total immersion in digital options but demands extraordinary skills before picking almost freely available options. No matter how small or how global your ideas may appear to be, this is where all things begin and end. When right expertise meeting right and almost free technologies meet creative fireworks, the entrepreneurial streaks will shine. Otherwise darkness.

To be successful in today's digital world organizations must open their mind and accept this global age style thinking. With practice it becomes easy. The majority of our free-flow, but refined and organized dreams can become reality with almost free-flow technologies, provided, self-discovery and self-optimization have already uncluttered the mind, refreshed the body and cleared paths to expedient decision making. All the heavy lifting is done by your mind, now waiting for you to advance and create real value. All it takes is internal adjustments and having the will to make peace with your mind and lead change. Embrace technology at each and every sliced and sectional aspect of your ideas or enterprise

Action call: To build anything, whether, big or small, goods or services, local or global, enterprises thinking must dream with automated interactive global accessibility included at every step. Those dreams must figure out how to connect and link billions of others and millions of other enterprises across multi-continental landscapes. Now slowly start transforming dreams into realities; it may take weeks, months or years. It makes no difference because, as your mind blends with technology, you will find amazing solutions. Crush all of the old thinking and bureaucracy embedded around you, and use your new powers of vision as your own powerful building platforms.

Now understanding the big picture. Because no organization of any kind, size or location anywhere in the world will survive or grow without in-depth understanding of all the new meanings, definitions and pragmatic deployments of technology, these factors must be completely understood. It's not about becoming an IT expert but rather about becoming technology minded.

Imagine, the internet as a bulb, something that 100 years ago was bright enough to kindle the industrial revolution. Now with AI and E-commerce the internet will light up the world of commerce like a Christmas tree. The internet will continue this kindle and grow like a bonfire as a new revolution. Smartness of ideas and speedy execution will determine success.

These new boundary-less, intricate, global business practices will either make you instantly a super success or they will crush your empire in a slow death. Study Alibaba, study the downfall of retail in developed countries.

A new world of mega winners is approaching. The world is wide open with endless boulevards of opportunities lined up on both sides of the boulevard and ready for action. Decades ago we went to trade shows to find customers; today there are five billion customers online and searching for what you have to offer.

The around-the-clock global races for national image supremacy make, conventional 9-5 working model and local thinking, obsolete. These global, time sensitive races have already shrunken the overstretched Julian calendar-based timelines and make organizational demands for weekends, seasonal breaks, holidays all out dated and unproductive. A new world of non-stop execution and super speed action become a new norm. Imagine month- long shut downs of plants and slow-mode seasonal office routines as a thing of the past. There is no such thing as 9-5 but rather 24 hours of constant 'sun rises' somewhere around the world.

The new global organizational time-zone thinking is not about having your entire staff chained to the office and factory walls for the full year, on the contrary make them work less, but work-smarter, distribute shifts, make holidays and weekend teams, create new shift jobs, make an organization that is alive all the time and it's staffing selected and managed as such with great personal and health care for better performance. This is new thinking, good-bye old HR. Rediscover global age human talent management and place business cards in the garbage.

Technocalamity is now a reality. Skill gaps issues demand proof of new global age literacy in order to have qualified leaders at the helm. Across the globe there are hundreds of millions of unprepared businesses demonstrating the lack of practice, absence of engagement, and organization-wide mediocrity in their relative market places. Their domestic economies are also losing their edge on a fast track. The export expansion races amongst nations are increasingly tough and only the very best will survive.

Questions no one dares to ask and why they must be answered. How global-age-internet-street-literate do we have to be? Why is there is so much tension, confusion and disconnect amongst leaders of businesses all over the world? Either the processes have become too complicated or we lack advance literacy of global age issues and Technocalamity. During the Print Society in the 1900s, when printed words were power, only the privileged had access to the printed knowledge access providing powers, the privileged were the literate of the day. Now, 120 years later as technologically advances and artificial intelligence starts controlling improved processes, knowledge is only to the highly literate who read between the lines and connect the dots, while the rest of the population watches as amazed spectators. For the dreamers of new ideas, it's more about technological minds and entrepreneurial spirits and not necessarily about collecting IT degrees. Will universities be able provide the required results? Entrepreneurs are feared for being out of box thinkers. Today the 'world' is outside the box. Today nations without smart leadership on entrepreneurialism are 'under the box'. Now Deployment of Technocalamity – massive global advantage. Are you afraid of a detailed audit or a critical assessment?

Three Internal Audits

Internal audit one: Reflections of a diamond. Now you have a brilliant idea; the original thinking and precise evaluation of each and every process from design and manufacturing to marketing and distribution; identify all critical touch points, juxtaposed to various types of digital inter-phases, mostly available for free or at little costs, but enlarge global access, portability and replication. This process is not capital intense, rather it is global knowledge centric and not to be confused to a typical re-engineering exercise. It is rather a new digital age tango. Where image supremacy of innovative excellence collides with powerful vision and solid ideas ready for execution. This process can take 365 hours to 365 days but depending on the right combinations, ideas and mental stamina. Most importantly, if carried out with commanding knowledge, it can quadruple the business growth, profitability, and market positioning.

Internal audit two: Missing skills. Evaluate each and every process of human interaction juxtaposed to all digital touch points based on new and widely enlarged potential global landscapes. People will be realigned and re-positioned based on their extreme skills, convictions and goals. This is not a typical HR exercise but rather a deep philosophical understanding of Technocalamity and how skill gaps are currently imploding organization. Workers are becoming redundant for not working hard enough, but their refusal to not optimize their talent with digital, global age thinking, knowledge and execution. Most importantly the entire organization requires this immersion and just revamping IT department will not solve the challenge. The process can take two days to two months but it will dramatically streamline the organization and prepare it for new expansion surrounded with Technocalamity

Internal audit three: Crystallization of vision. A proof is required to verify if vison is crystal clear and not to be confused with illusion or worst any kind of hallucination. The isolation of the corporate fundamentalism, which is the idiotic stubbornness of not adopting new game changing plans, because the fresh new ideas will eliminate the silos of the last century. This is not a closed-door leadership evaluation, but rather a very bold, interactive challenge to vision and its driving forces. Without clarity, fog will keep all aspects of the organization in a tunnel. This process never ends and requires frequent visits. The results are so obvious. Winning is assured. Though such ideas are so simple and common-sense, the majority of organizations are petrified to even think about them, much less go through such progressive developments. Under proper and trained leadership such open and engaging discussions and debates create positive crystallization of vison for all to touch and feel the reality and fully comprehend the dimensions and deployment strategies. It's highly recommended for top leadership to commit to few days a year as a mandatory annual program.

A twenty-twenty faceted future unfolds

As 9-5 office work disappears, downtown skyscrapers will lose their grip in smaller cities. The corporate centrality of new routines and habits will impact 'on-demand productivity' and 'shared services' will cascade. These new routines eliminate the concepts of typical office jobs, weekly payroll and bureaucratic hierarchies. This transformation will be like advancing the ever-growing 'gig economy'. This economy will thrive amongst the cluster of on-demand, online, skill exchanges, making the 'self-trained', 'self-employed' and 'self-occupied' the largest working groups. Just like a gemologist can better appreciate the cut of a diamond, a mastery of global age understanding is a prerequisite to deciphering and unfolding of a multi-faceted future.

ction: study deeply, become comfortable, become technically minded and execute with global visions in mind; remember most technology is almost free; it's all in the creative art and entrepreneurial disciplines on how capitalize on Technocalamity

While on the other side, the age of abundance will continuously drown mediocrity and shred weaker business models, the constant overflow of great globally accessible and affordable ideas will crush parochial think-ing and single-sided nationalism. The global-age culture will dominate and force reevaluation of everything. Superstar entrepreneurialism will be the most desired model.

Refinements and execution models to build new ideas. Make a list of technologies you already know and then search on Google and match what you learn against what each technology sector has already achieved and how fast it is advancing. It's a mind blowing and extremely powerful exercise especially if some of the dots were to fit your idea's direction.

This should be a regular exercise. Depending on types and styles of applications most of these new advancements are almost free. If properly deployed they will take you to upper stratosphere in no time. This understanding is very critical because if this happens you could get sucked into a downward vortex or rise for blue skies. The rest is up to you. Enjoy the ride.

To do lists

If you are currently not an IT person, please try not to become one just to be able to stay alive in technocalamity. There is no need, as there are billion IT experts of sorts, all you need is to develop a technical mind to appreciate, understand and listen, work with specialists of sorts; because when you have a heart issue you do not become a Cardiologist, you just develop a healthy body and cognizance to what makes a healthy heart.

If you have old technology do not panic to buy new technology in a box, rather re-invent your entire business model based on technology. This demands advanced study. Technology is going to change faster than the growth of your business and your cycle of change. On this basis you will be always behind. Try to differentiate between models and types of technologies, the gadget side and the guts and platform side. Stay to your core competencies, but surround yourself with technology experts. Adoption of technology is easiest when you become wise about technology and not a trendy-adapter.

If your markets are all going in one direction in technology adoption be bold and explore opposite directions, also do not adopt for tomorrow rather for the day after tomorrow.

If you are locally focused, you may be missing on everything, as a business of any type with technology you are automatically a fish in a very large ocean, get out of your pond. If you are national, articulate very clearly what's stopping you from becoming global and what do you really need to become one. Money is often the smallest part, creating global positioning, identity and procedural controls are the real issues. The rest is easy.

For all your large or small teams make a point to have just technology focused regular meetings and make sure that they not about techno-lingo, but about touch points of the operations from start to finish with massive consideration of the customers who are often armed from top to bottom with gadgets and expecting instant service.

If you are multi-talented and technology is also one of your key strengths, you are now unstoppable and the world awaits you. Redesign your high-quality global models and do not look back.

Technology Test

What you do not know is not important, what you already know is far more valuable

List all the possible options you can imagine about what new technology can do for you today

What can you imagine, what would you ideally like to happen?

What, where, when and how it will be done?

Who will help, who will build, who will test, who will benefit?

Where is all this hidden, when will all this be discovered?

Who will pay what cost, what it has do with bottom-line and market-share?

Why I'm not doing it today?

Chapter Nine

**Only repetitive and continuous refinements will get you the spotlight;
one time wonders only make back pages of local community papers**

Strategy two: Age of abundance

Definition: Age of Abundance has followed the age of curiosity and scarcity; we are in the age of abundance, where for every great idea, we have thousands of better ones.

Usage: build any new idea with extreme uniqueness and high value design.

Symptoms: PR, promotional campaigns are up but sales are down; competition has better, faster, cheaper options; the race is being lost; victory is hidden in other brand-new strategies; vision is being challenged, and the fog of confusion is cutting profits.

How to design a new idea

Should we become overly content with whatever quality we produce? Without a full grasp of the age of abundance one cannot think, design or produce anything, period. Study design from all aspects, for example, like from a car designer's point of view and also from you sitting in a driver seat point of view; go line by line, item by item, study every corner, every feature, and every grain and ask how and why it was done in that manner or why it was not done. Now do this for 100 other major products and you will start to develop a third eye for design appreciation.

You need not to be a car designer or artificial heart maker, that's for other experts to step in, you are a builder and your deep appreciation is far more important in order to engage with other experts along the way. While your skills are much wider, even generic but driven by unique forces of entrepreneurialism, execution and out of box thinking will assure you are on the path of discovery. You are a builder; you deal with everything and as you have the right skills. Design thinking must o parallel with your progress. Study all the success stories, now restudy from the design point of view.

What's age of abundance; visit the largest shopping mall, multiply it by a million more malls and it's still not big enough… the new global age is over-flooded with everything, good and bad, mediocre and excellent, junk and collector's items. Without understanding the Age of Abundance, any idea, no matter what must create extreme value and extreme image otherwise it's simply doomed from the start. If you wish to make a spicy sauce, you must study the 10,000 sauces that are already available. You must check the labels, sizes, shapes, prices and sample flavors. The same applies to socks, scarves, cars, motorbikes, music, food, clothing, books, drones, movies, seminars, high-speed-trains and just about anything.

This does not mean that there is nothing left to do…on the contrary this is a limitless market. If there is good knowledge of innovative design with extreme value and extreme image, there will be success. There is so much junk and nonsensical designs and images that it automatically open millions of new doors for high quality contributions.

Design: this require special training to deeply understand the various and multiple dimensions of design, the philosophy, the school and the styles. Without such knowledge most ideas of goods and services miserably suffer a slow death.

Production: produce if you can, collaborate if you can, outsourcing with command and control of design is the fastest way to global age markets

Promise: how to create and how to deliver the promise is a fine art, requires mastery

Timing: today it's all about timing, being at the right place with the right combination at the right time. This also means being fast and extremely efficient, something that requires special skills.

Competition: despite the flooded markets, if you have mastery of all of these components, there is hardly any competition who have the combinations needed for success.

Consumption: how things move from factory floors to consumers; any idea without solid marketing, local and global accessibility will simply die.

Image supremacy: the age of abundance allows the best of the best to climb to the top. However, it will only allow experts with mastery to even enter the race.

Basically, the cup of consumption runneth over; the consumer and consumee are both drunk on liquid plastic fumes and stagger towards the horizon, while the 'bunga bunga' parties isolate the bureautoxicated incompetent debt builders and collect their awards of merits. The Future of the Age of Abundance is abundantly clear and points to fake economies and debt centric false sense of prosperity.

Three critical progressive stages were originally defined

Age of Curiosity: here, for anything newly created or produced there were either one or a few other options. Access to originality and production was extremely rare.

Age of Scarcity: here, for anything produced there were hundreds of other options. Access to production and easy replication was very common.

Age of Abundance: when, for anything produced or created there are thousands or millions of other options. Access to production, replication and global distribution is in abundance.

Choice Attacks: When there are millions of choices and options, there is an automatic sense of rejection. Elvin Toffler defined Future Shock in the eighties. Now we can walk into a Mega-Mall-Mega-Mart which creates 'choice attack' as the mind refuses to process the subtle culinary desires and the emotional awakening of imaginary pots and pan. Selecting a cooking sauce from 100 plus varieties shuts down all the excitement and creates massive abundance of agoraphobia forcing a person to hyperventilate and run out of the store in a panic. In times past, guards controlled the onslaught of incoming customers; now in the age of abundance, there are guards inside the store so that customers simply don't run out screaming due to 'choice attacks.

The Origin: *The concept of the 'age of abundance' was originally published in a syndicated column "The Age of Abundance Demands Innovation" by Naseem Javed in 2005.*

The new problematic challenges; The new human talent calibrations in age of abundance. As we are trapped in the age of abundance, we are daily bombarded and find we must learn new ways to alter and manage our own talent.

HR-Human Resource is becoming obsolete. It is an old term related to the organizational structuring of bureaucracies. Today we must think in terms of TM-Talent Management, were we are shifting to the management of extreme mental agility of entrepreneurially pragmatic global age deployments. HR mentality hires people to fit job descriptions and misses out on hidden talent. In today's world, it's less about procedures and job description and more about out of the box liberation and smart execution. ASK NOT why are you performing so perfectly to your job descriptions, but RATHER ASK what you are not doing that was never asked from you or what you were not hired for?

This notion alone is creating sleepless nights and serious health problems amongst management. To tackle such fears of insecurities and uncertainties, brand new measurement systems must be deployed. Massive unlearning to cope with Technocalamity and alpha dreamer lifestyle must be introduced. The future is hidden in entrepreneurialism and NOT in corporate bureaucracies.

Fact: Human brains are capable to invent the powerful machines that surpass our bodily strengths, as our bodies can never compete with such power-machines. Humans were unable to fly but very capable of inventing the Jumbo jet planes. Today we have invented sophistication in our technologies that our mind alone cannot keep pace with. Now we cannot survive without full technology support and functionalities. Executives have done an amazing job pushing technology to the point to make themselves redundant. New HR views are needed and mental divides filled.

On the other hand, if the lions of the jungle got room service three times a day, will they stop hunting and pick up bird watching or learn to swim with dolphins? No!

Billions of unemployed executives of the new futures are still the lions in search of the game. They have the richness of experience and all the necessary qualifications from the past; the missing link is the new global age transformation into entrepreneurial thinking. In the past such addition of new skills was considered impossible, but now these challenges can be solved with massive learning deployments. They will slowly let the procedural roles go and relearn new entrepreneurial platforms, where these engagements will revitalize the organizations.

The biggest assets of a nation are hidden in their entrepreneurial spirits and only those national leaderships that can boldly show case a deeper understanding and respect to entrepreneurial thinking will survive. During the last decades such entrepreneurial notions were crushed over other fake priorities and led to economic collapse for many developed nations.

Global age thinking: = machine power=brain power=execution power

TEST ONE: Imagine a fully developed mature and successful organization, fully automated, 100% running via AI and massive digitalization. Top to bottom, the organization operates without any staff of any kind. It would look a lot like a Sci Fi movie. Now further imagine, you will see their top 1000 senior and middle management going crazy and in a state of shock, boredom and anxiety, all combined under the big umbrella of their own unexplainable insecurities and panic as their own performances and skills are being constantly measured against machines. Kindly stay here, indulge deeper; can you see them running around corridors and going up and down elevators like zombies. This is what has started to happen in mega organizations as Technocalamity over takes human performance. The majorities of these executives have very little or zero understanding of how such massive automation is operated, because to them that's a different IT area and outside the realm of conventional expertise or job descriptions.

TEST TWO: Imagine 1000 executives, having little or no influence on how their mammoth organizations, mostly AI and metadata, are driven. Now further imagine the same 1000 executives given large white sheets and crayons in order to invent new business models based on what they know. The will doodle and crawl out amazing and astonishing ideas. At times ten times better and faster models than what the currently AI Mata data centric organization is already doing. This is lions hunting. Executives should never be afraid of robotics and automation but should be terrified of their own incompetence for not having high level emotional and intellectual capital and special skills learning to survive such advanced levels of business modelling.

Fact: The human mind is the most amazing phenomena of our universe. The mind is akin to a large forest, while our modern claims to artificial intelligence with global Meta-Data and is just a single termite in that forest. On technology performance side, millions of workers searching zillions of index cards to answer a single query could never match man-made Google. On human intuitiveness side, the human mind on the business prosperity and economical models basically was abused and abandoned in our dysfunctional models. However, the mind is far too capable to ignore the noise of confusion; it is able and ready for far bigger and better things.

All these demands unlearning and relearning. The upper-strata of human performance and intelligence cannot be easily fixed. This requires very special methodologies. It can be transformed with the real truth and global age affairs.

Liberate the human intelligence: It is time to free the untapped flow of ideas and help an entire organization achieve the image supremacy of thoughtful leadership and innovative excellence. During the last few decades the corporate models, instead of becoming cathedrals of advanced thinking and working models they become more like potato farms of mental silo storages where bickering, back-stabbing and constant harassment became the norm. No amount of flatbed thinking, psychological and stress treatment will work unless new global issues are brought to the forefront. HR has badly failed in such fronts. Fear of losing job titles the corporate corridors bury such issues.

Discover the best minds and talents hidden behind job titles on wrong floors.

Creating Extreme Value: Survival Strategy

Nobility and aristocracy were both decimated during the horse and donkey days of the renaissance when smartness was deployed along with homing pigeons. The supremacy of information gathering was established. Extreme value was created.

During every century, on the business front, the power of establishment and wealth gets less and less important. What becomes important is the speed and styles of execution. A deeper study of game disruption provides the proof. Technocalamity creates fear, takes over daily procedures and creates emptiness; it can be filled with either by bureaucracy or by innovative excellence and entrepreneurialism, provided the corporate leadership clearly understands the difference and the grasp of new global age battlefields.

We are drowning and now we need life guards. It is time to kill overly duplicated concepts and stop staying lost in massive copycat clutter. Nurture originality, quality and extreme value creation will lead to success. Eliminate extreme value manipulation. Stop the over packaging of undervalued goods. Think three times before consumption; ask each time if it's really necessary. Think ten times before production and continually as if it's of real, real, real value--worthy of production.

This is where extreme value creation emerges and innovative excellence starts breeding. In this frame of mind, now the survival of the fittest is no longer measured by being first or big in the marketplace, but by being extremely unique and highly strategic all the way. It involves demonstration of image supremacy and innovative excellence. In this age of abundance unlimited opportunities really belong to the very smart and timely executions. A very bright future waits for the Bolden.

Idea-Designing to get an edge in the global 'age of abundance'

Refinements and execution models to build new ideas

Find the world's largest malls and get lost inside. Do it in person or do it online, but develop a deep sense of size and scope of what the world is producing, consuming and how it is dancing. Now bring this knowledge back to your invention. Be it a paper clip or a Jumbo Jet... it's all about deeper understanding of design, value, features and advanced appreciation of end users thinking. This can take years or decades

Chapter Ten

Silence of the machines proves entrapments of hard assets mentality
Silence of the mind proves optimization of soft assets management

Strategy Three: Soft-power-assets management

Definition: Soft-power assets are invisible assets such as vision, imagination and creative entrepreneurial skills.

Usage: build with creativity and wild imagination, like using steel and cement to hold a skyscraper.

Symptoms: Massive structural sets up now appear outdated, no new options, formulations and methodologies now appear liabilities, constant cost cutting will undermine stability, massive shift is new skills and strategies a must.

Build ideas like using solid steel and cemented structures

Should we only regard our hardware and factories as our only assets?

Close your eyes and try hard to forget whatever you see in front of you in the office or factory floors; now let your imagination grow and dream of whatever comes to mind as possible brand new ideas, new products and services and how will they be made, distributed and exported; do this as many times as you like as you are getting into soft-power-asset-management thinking mode. Sometime in this journey you will discover things that were completely missed previously. But to be a leader in these thought processes you must not ignore all the other key ingredients of building to make your day dreaming closer to realities. Dream but make those dreams meaningful and tangible; dream but make your entrepreneurial imagination reach the sky. Pay less attention to hard structures around you, dream of new ideas outside such constraints.

The future is all about our inner-strengths, though invisible and hidden with our untapped and undiscovered consciousness as this is where our expressions on prosperity and harmonious growth are hidden. Use imagination and innovative thinking as your steel and cement.

Soft power asset management is about issues related to vision, imagination, innovation, talent and execution, and when calibrated by applying special methodologies three dimensional views appear. With tweaking such configuration can catapult new innovative ideas to upper the stratosphere, resulting in achieving image supremacy of performance and innovative excellence.

In order to understand soft-power-assets, we must look in contrast to hard-assets-centricity. It's all about what we see in front of us, the office-floors or factory-floors and concentrating on what we see inside the box does not allow us to observe current reality and we do not allow ourselves to go outside the box.

Try hard to see but with your mind, not just eyes alone.

Hard asset centricity is all about the daily grind of life, surrounded by work from offices to productions, manufacturing or being locked into procedural and structural binds, unable to change but still forcing the hard structures to become moveable but often without much progress. This is why millions of businesses around the world who were once on the right trajectory are now so off target and in a downward tail spin?

There are multiple reasons but most hidden are the tectonic shifts towards soft asset management.

Today's world is changing so fast that by the time your latest factory opens most of its hard assets are on their way to obsoleteness; change in technology, global age pricing access, end-user's accessibility and upcoming monster trends push those ideas into the outdated files. Therefore, soft power asset management provides the ultimate flexibility and deploys vision, imagination and talent as the main differentiators over raw production and prices. The subject requires a deeper understanding especially when the global mind set is so comfortably nestled in 'hard asset centricity'.

Idea-Cementing with steel

Ideas need substance, power and weight, otherwise they are fly-by-night dreams. Their growth and execution demand cement and steel otherwise the structure would collapse. To allow an idea to grow and spread wings requires 'soft-power-asset-management'; this is how to handle imagination, creativity and vision; this is about allowing the mind to do all the heavy lifting. During the old days, 'hard-asset-centricity' mode, basically whatever we dealt on the basis what's in front of us, factory floors, inventory and warehouses, whatever was visible. Today, we must deal with soft-power-asset-management which deals with the invisible side. Would you create a factory to make a wheel for your bicycle production or would you design aerodynamic structure and outsource or create partnerships with wheel makers for a creative production for all? Creative structuring and using soft-power-asset deployments is the fastest way to grow national or global projects. As more machines and smart technologies take over development of such forces as calibrated thinking, organized imagination, and crystallization of vision is where the growth genius is hidden.

Study how skyscrapers are built. Study how your dreams are structured and keep on studying all of the time; you will start finding steel and cement all around you and you are now on the right path.

The hard and soft thinking

Back in the last century, if you were the CEO of a major Fortune 500 organization, you commanded from your huge office from the very top floor of one of the tallest skyscrapers in the city. As the oxygen of the organization was sucked upward, you and the rest of the team knew with certainty that this was the center of the universe. Of course, this worked wonders, and this format also provided the best of the best business minds to deploy the best 'hard asset' strategies of the period.

Hard asset thinking is a state of mind where the mind acts like a goal keeper, catching nicely baked generic ideas as they are shot into the net. Hard asset centricity played a key role; it built factories to produce and move goods. The hard mentalists applied special skills sets to deflect some ideas but catching the right projectiles. The execution styles were based on choosing the right hard asset-based strategies from the very top floor and trickling those ideas as downward flows. The land was hungry and too many great ideas were flying around like bees. The happy dawn of America and Western image supremacy was assured on the Hard asset thinking clock. Soft asset is a state of limitless, boundary less, timeless free flow thinking on 'soft power asset management' issues. In this new global age, it's more about the unique mental stamina needed to process all kinds and types of information, with hundreds of interactions going on at the same time. The parties involved are scattered all over the nation or globe and challenges are processed in real time. Month long trips and seasonal reviews will give way to answering questions and solving issues in one single day and frequently every single day. In such massive innovative thinking, old knowledge skills would end up flying like a lost mosquito randomly searching for a bite.

New Soft asset thinking has its own digital intellectualism intertwined with global age thinking and executions skills. Once the creative dreams get properly aligned and the latter-day hard asset management teams actually start constructing the dreams, the entire business model successfully gets tested in real time well in advance with soft-power execution.

Chapter Eleven

Plan the planning for perpetual planning

Strategy Four: Equation 365=365

Definition: how to achieve in 365 hours what we are conditioned to achieve in 365 days.

Usage: create high speed performance by new thinking of time and optimization, like high speed elevators work in skyscrapers.

Symptoms: For every new thrust in markets competition, the markets are always few steps ahead; long cycles of innovative thinking are hurting the organization; traditionally sluggish operation needs new definitions and new behavior to survive

The hyper speed of execution

Should we accept our current speed of progress as top standard?

Discover time equation how to achieve in 365 hours what we normally achieve in 365 days. This is about achieving results at an extraordinary speed which is like creating high-speed elevators in the towering organization to make it superfast agile like an active living organism. This also requires very special and serious training to understand how to achieve in 365 hours what we are normally conditioned to achieve in 365 days. Just imagine the power of an organization that thinks, operates and functions like this, no matter of its size, location, or type of industry. Consider what could be accomplished with the power of speed deployed correctly across the organization and when all the prime teams are simultaneously working on these principles.

To increase super performance and productivity, you must think tactically to go from point A to B. Sometimes, it is best to put the calendar away and ask all teams three questions.

This is the time to think freely and let minds explore. Challenge the team on two aspects, what will be the consequence of this one-year project if it was done in even at 10% of time? What will be the real value? Seek out options and scenarios. Is the entire team, trained and ready to tackle and willing to experiment in total synchronization? Self-discovery and self-optimization will teach you how to chart all this out and asses the big picture, costs, timelines, teamwork, corporate issues and possible results. Without this little will make sense.

Let's say you come up on a project like 'opening three overseas markets', or 'doubling sales by increasing your national presence' or 'organizing a major conference on your specific trade issues' each or all of the three must be completed in an already tight and busy schedule during the next 300 days. Now, as a start, let's do it in 30 days as a training exercise.

Firstly, all team members must be fully prepared on the self-discovery and self-optimization and would agree to ignore the clocks and calendars. Lock the team for 2-3 days where they concentrate only on this. Ask every single question on every single thing, line by line, on each of the single step of each and every aspect of each project and bring all into real time basis and measure the actual time to process. With this slicing and dicing, immediately multiple options as many new time-lines will start to appear. After a few such projects this part will become a very logical exercise. The objective is not to rush, neither to save payroll, nor make errors and sacrifice quality. The bottom line is if it can be done then what's stopping it from occurring on a regular basis. What if this speed will provide a powerful tool on performance and competitive advantage? What if the time saving is also almost creating new cash-flow and better profitability?

For example, how long should it take to invent a brand-new style of bicycle?

Should it be five years, five months or five weeks? Each timeline has its unique demands. But smart age thinking can do it in the minimal timeline with maximum output. Traditional thinking would settle for five years to play safe and to appear comfortably normal. The more zealous thinking would go for five months. The global age smartness would get the best designers and create an outsourced model to have a prototype figured out in few weeks. Of course, this is just an imaginary exercise on how to achieve in 365 hours where we normally waste in 365 days. However, in the end, it's more about attitude and performance, both tackled via self-discovery and self-optimization. The leadership plus prime teams must go through in-depth self-discovery. Starting training and intense appreciation in what minds can do when allows for freely entangle and seeks soft-power-asset-management. Such subjects, thinking and execution will not be found in the top Business-Schools curriculum because this type of thinking is too entrepreneurial and drastically advanced.

Three quick methodologies will get you started: First create lists of each single action on each program, completely broken down with key assignments. Then identify execution paths with expertise hunts to make all things go on instant response basis. Third start timeline coordination to create real time supply chain on performance. This requires repeated practice depending on type of projects.

Results: Given the right combinations for a project spanned over 300 days most of this super-compressed planning and execution over 2-3 intense days may narrow it all down to a 30-day timeline but with many variables and questions. Depending on the situation, the exercise will definitely prove very significant and many brand-new ideas and strategies will emerge. The biggest challenges will be the leadership to drive and the team to engage. The project will be successful if it is an entrepreneurially driven task and it will lead to a dead end if it is managed as a cost saving project or a 'time and motion' study. If the execution and delivery of items are in place, you will discover that it can be done and it will certainly be worth a try. If the team handles a few such campaigns it will change the picture across the organization. The message; destroy old thinking and bureaucracies, the attitudes of old style and start looking at organizational issues with global age mind. Nothing ventured, nothing gained; it is time to give this type of thinking a try. It's all about what can be done and not how it's done.

The big question is why it was never done before. The answer is probably because no one in the organization ever believed that it was possible. The world has changed and only if you try 360 turns it starts making sense. Ten such attempts and soon you will realize that majority of the work normally taking a year's work can be achieved in 10% or 35 days and eventually in 1 % or 3 days. This is about new style thinking and new expectations.

Observe the current standards from the last century. Long boring reports and studies were passed around to senior management with normal response rates of 1-2 weeks. Try instead editing to two pages and asking for response on the same day.

Complex decisions linger and take time, normally on monthly cycles, and can further linger for months if intersected by 'annual budgets' or summer breaks. Create a culture where complex issues are tackled within 48 hours.

Outside dealings are based on complex delays and are as part of doing business. It will be better to require responses to your issues be completed within 24 hours.

The issues here are not that crazy. In Fact, these ideas can happen; the question is, why are they not being used?

The bottom line is that bureaucracy over decades have created open or deep web of delays as job security. Either reward your snail pace crawl or re-create a new job-security culture where extreme performance with speed becomes new standard.

This execution style and thinking may possibly get you into serious trouble; the more an organization is set in old styles the harder your new deployments will become. It will also require special skills in communications and team building. Today, it's an art to survive in a large dwindling organization and to top it off by trying to bring such new dramatic thinking is the fastest way to get fired.

Therefore, self-discovery and self-optimization are over and above any job and far more valuable because it creates a superior level of new confidence with new opportunities. Smart management will immediately recognize smart team players.

Beneficiaries: Those arms of the organization that wish to advance without new funding and use speed to turn the performance as new profit and competitive advantage and those who like to achieve spotlight on themselves and their project.

Enemies: Those who believe if the work can shrink by 90%, they may also lose 90% of staffing-hours and those who believe that management may blame them for being slow all these times and those who believe that why kill yourself if slow and steady is the best and humdrum way of lingering in the markets.

Adjustments: bring out new policies to credit smart work over hard work and give unlimited time off to staff as long they meet deadlines. Create a bonus system where timelines targeting is rewarded.

Advanced thinking

Study the last three years and think of the years in terms of day by day progress. Remember the old day timers for example and begin to question each move and rewrite a new plan that might have been implemented. You will immediately start with 10 to 50% of time saving ideas. Now that you get the ideas, start some serious note keeping and question everything so you can take a quantum leap and then you will be on the right track

Dairies are far more important to analyze the past than to plan ahead... planning ahead is old habit based, past analysis is new learning

The real tasks

Consider if you could do every other task in 1% of its required time. How much better would you be? At first this may seem an impossibility, but later when it becomes a reality you will become a very special performer.

Consider this example; if a driving trip takes 100 minutes there is no need for dangerous speeding to arrive in one minute. However, think of eliminating drive all together. It may not work immediately, but it may become a creative option down the road. For example, a deeply researched report takes 100 days to complete but ask very tough questions of the real value of the report going forward months in the future. Maybe there are better ways to communicate the report information. If the report is essential, double the task and teams for the report and determine if it would really save 10,000 days somewhere else. Ask difficult questions but focus on time wastage. You will easily find 20%-50% of wasted time. Normally, examples such as this are pushed under corporate corridor and hush hushed under carpets of political correctness. Time demands can be compressed. Bureaucracy is when small or big tasks time requirement are stretched to infinity and the sound of stillness appears as music to numbing minds suffering dependency to slow speed; this is how being busy gets considered avant-garde

Idea-expansion, via speed of planning and execution as critical edge. This is about achieving results at an extraordinary speed; it is like creating high-speed elevators in the towering organizations in order to make them superfast, agile and active living organism. This also requires a very special and serious way of thinking in order to understand how to achieve in 365 hours what we have normally accomplished in 365 days.

Just imagine the power of this type of thinking and attainment for organizations-- no matter of its size, location, type or industry. Picture the power of this speed when deployed by your organization and the influence your prime teams achieve while working within these principles.

Three big questions

Questions: How immediately can a problem be solved and what will it require to make this happen. Here with thinking-freely determine the actual tasks and exact requirements needed and then tackle them simultaneously. Practice is required.

Questions: What will really happen if success happens and what will happen if it doesn't happen? We must seek options and explore scenarios. Is the entire team ready to tackle the challenges involved and is willing to experiment in total synchronization?

Questions: Self-discovery and self-optimization will lead to answers and ways to chart through the steps needed for success. It is essential that we see the big picture in terms of assets, costs, timelines, teams and their issues, corporate issues and possible results. Without seeing the big picture of how all of these factors interact, little will make sense.

For example, let's assume you come up with a project for opening three overseas markets plus an idea for doubling sales by increasing your national presence plus a plan for organizing a major conference on your specific trade issues; whether one item or all three together supposed to be visualized and completed in light of already tight and a busy schedule over the next 300 days. Now, as a start, let's do all of it in 30 days as an extensive facilitated exercise.

Firstly, all team members must be fully prepared, able to apply the self-discovery and self-optimization and agree to ignore the clocks and calendars. Lock the team together for 2-3 days so they can plan uninterrupted and focus on the ideas. The process begins by asking every possible question on every single part of the ideas line by line. By evaluating each step of each and every aspect of each project in real time and all aspects of the ideas will be calculated in terms of time and overall effect on the organization. With this slicing and dicing approach, immediately multiple options and new time lines will come together. After a few of these very logical exercises, such projects with hyper-speed will become second nature. The objective is not to rush through the project just to save payroll or to move too quickly and make errors or sacrifice quality. The bottom line is if it can be done then nothing should stop it. This process will provide a powerful tool on performance and competitive advantage? At the same time, it can create new cash-flow and increased profitability. Faster time to new products, new customers, new results, without prolonged overheads = better cash flows.

For example, how long should it take to invent a brand-new style of bicycle?

Should this new bicycle take five years, five months or five weeks? Each timeline has its unique demands. Smart age thinking can do it in the minimal timeline with maximum output. Traditional thinking would settle for five years in order to play it safe, where more zealous thinking would go for five months. Global age smartness would get the best designers and create an outsourced model to have a prototype available in a few weeks. This is just an imaginary exercise on how to achieve in 365 hours what we normally waste in 365 days. However, in the end, it's more about attitude and performance. Both tackled via self-discovery and -self optimization will lead to increased achievement. Leadership working with prime teams must be able to thoroughly understand and apply in-depth self-discovery. Applying these concepts involves intense appreciation and practice of what minds can do when allowed to freely tangle and seek soft-power-asset-management possibilities. Such subjects, thinking and execution will NOT be found in a university curriculum. Execution is entrepreneurial and drastically advanced and will only come to reality through the application of deep thinking and exploration techniques.

Three quick methodologies begin the process. The first involves master lists creation of each single action on each program, constantly broken down with key assignments. Then we must identify execution paths with expertise hunting approaches in order to make all aspects respond with on an instant response basis. The third part involves timeline coordination in order to create real time supply chain on performance

Results: Given the right combinations for a project that would span over 300 days, with this 2-3 super-compressed planning and execution can easily be completed within a 30-day or less timeline. However, it will take many variables and questions. Depending on the situation, the exercise will definitely prove to be very significant in terms of time and economic savings; and more importantly many brand-new ideas and strategies will be presented and evaluated. The biggest challenges will be for leadership to drive and engage the team. Also, this is an entrepreneurially driven task and not a heavily managed cost saving project management or a 'time and motion' study. If the execution and delivery of items are in place, you will discover that it can be done efficiently and it is certainly worth a try. The results are powerful and if the team only handles a few such campaigns, it will change the picture across the organization. The message, destroy old thinking and bureaucracies, throw out the attitudes of old-style leadership and start looking at the organization with global age eyes and global age mind exploration. Nothing ventured, nothing gained.

The big lesson is to ask why it was not done in the past and is not being done now. It is simple, no one in the organization ever believed that it was possible. The world has changed and your organization will change with it only if you take advantage of the world's 360-degrees turns. Once you step into this 360 turning world, it will start making sense. Ten such attempts and you will realize that this new approach works. What was normally taking a year's work can be achieved in 10% or 35 days and eventually in 1 % or 3 days. This is about a new style of thinking.

Observe; the current standards for leadership from the last century. Long boring paper reports and studies taking months are still passed around to senior management and response times can take weeks. For most organizations, complex decisions linger and are normally on monthly cycles. Some decisions can linger for months if intersected by 'annual budgets' or summer breaks. The organizations of today and tomorrow must create a culture where complex issues are tackled within 48 hours.

The bottom line is that bureaucracies over decades have created a deep web of delays with layers of complicated decision approvals, most without input or discussions. It led to job security and information protection, but it has not paid off in growth and increased prosperity. Either reward your snail pace crawl or re-create a new job-security culture with team involvement and where extreme performance with speed becomes the new standard.

This execution styles and thinking may get you into serious trouble; the more an organization is set in old styles, the harder your new deployments will become. It will also require special skills in communications and team building. Today, it's an art to survive in a large dwindling organization and introducing such new dramatic thinking might be the fastest way to get fired.

Therefore, self-discovery and self-optimization are more important than any job and far more valuable in creating superior level of new confidence, with new opportunities. Smart management will immediately recognize smart team players.

Beneficiaries: Those arms of the organization that wish to advance without new funding and use speed to turn performance into new profit and competitive advantage will prosper from this approach. Those who like to achieve spotlight for themselves, their project, and their organization will find that this tactic will make their business a star.

Enemies: Those who believe if the work can be completed with 90% less time may also feel they will lose 90% of staffing-hours. Those who believe that management may blame them for why being so slow all during the past. There are those who will ask why kill yourself if slow and steady gets things done. Those who are comfortable with the humdrum way of thinking and lingering in the markets is enough security and that change could lead to trouble.

Adjustments: bring out bold new policies to credit smart work over hard work; give unlimited time off to staff as long they meet deadlines, and create a bonus system where timelines targeting is rewarded.

The global age speed of execution

The new global age has no tolerance for sluggish performance. The new global age speed of execution demands mental stamina in order to align with the new ground realities of simultaneous speed of innovation with prosperity and all this in synchronization.

Why aren't you abundantly free?

Here are the two main reasons why the following types of people must be observed. Hard workers are basically hamsters aimlessly running on wheels; they are very busy processing what they did weeks or years ago, locked into traditional procedural thinking and believing in being busy. Technocalamity indicates leadership must learn to think, to adopt new free technologies to catapult operations in innovative excellence and growth. Lacking this wisdom and holding onto old style thinking of 'a solid day full of extreme hard work' will hurt them even more. It is time to create massive freedom and measure performance, and declare hard work as sign of deep trouble.

Type Two: Being busy is just stupid; being busy denies us the time needed to think. Too busy; busy people and managers suffer from 'busylepsy', a medical condition where unnecessary work is sequenced in a way to stretch all the available time to extreme limits of possibilities and artificially creating the feeling of importance. Real leaders are never too busy; they always demonstrate advanced level management skills and manage and delegate tasks with superb speed. They get results. Everyone has 24 hours each day. Every office manager and President of a super-power-nation have only 24 hours each day. Study this difference deeply. Being busy is a very old tradition, global age wisdom is about thinking, and thinking is not for busy people but for calm minds to do very heavy lifting but in weightless space.

Fact: The global consortiums of academically driven thought leadership responsible for mental gymnastics of coaching and psychological wisdom with performance measurement tools have not yet arrived at this stage.

Here is a test of smartness for key players in innovative growth and entrepreneurial excellence

Test:

How can we quadruple our performance with only 25% of working time?

How can we justify our position by deploying advance level execution for our entire organization?

How can we prove our worth ten times over our current pay rate?

How can we justify hooking a hammock in our office today and taking the rest of the week off, just to think?

Chapter Twelve

Hidden fortunes outside 9-5 working models of yesterday

Strategy Five: LIVE 24x7x365

Definition: how to create around the clock 24x7x365 organizational culture for global accessibility?

Usage: expand with new global age access and massive communication.

Symptoms: Local markets peaked, organizations cannot open dozens of new global age markets; retraining of the frontline delayed; processing of international business a nightmare, globally accessibility in crisis.

Globally accessible on 24x7x365 basis:

Should we be happily satisfied in a 9-5 working model? Why just survive when you can build for the world. Why not leap into this thinking because the world never sleeps but humans do. The global operations of big or small organization also never sleep, but if untrained in global age thinking, the majority of management will sleep. If we already live in 24x7x365 world and around the clock operations provide unlimited accessibility to engagements than what special skills and training are required to create such a system. Remember, this does not mean that the entire staff is sleeplessly working around the clock. This is not true at all. The organization is a structured in such a way that it is actively alive and engaging in professional responsive mode around-the-clock, seven days a week throughout the year. The organization is building ideas and expanding them in order to operate on that principle and knowing it is a remarkable achievement for our modern times.

Firstly, you must force your organization to unlearn the century old 9-5 model, Monday to Friday routines, or Sundays to Thursday routines. Ideas are for all to think about and your teams and organization, with the help of technologies, become a 24x7x365 operation. But they MUST know from the beginning that all teams will not work 24x7x365, rather all should work less and with much better-quality work and healthy mind.

Once again, massive charting and details of operation against desired overseas markets and their times zones will become paramount. Assemble a dozen team members anywhere in the world and 25% would be more than happy for the night shift or flexi hours. Imagine a group of 100 or a thousand. New stars discussing new options to engage live with overseas markets. Now explore language issues. Depending on countries, Western nations have large and trained bilingual and trilingual language people because of immigrants to such nations. In Toronto alone, a team of 100 will easily have over 50 languages spoken amongst them. Now start creating new timelines, new staff matching and HR issues. Reward and bonuses and bring the latest but almost free technologies on these stages to make the jobs and connectivity and recordkeeping easy for all. After a few months of struggle, an operation may get surprising results and become global age friendly, opening brand new territories. Nothing ventured, nothing gained, once again, it's all about unlearning the office clock.

Dancing with a wide-open world

Have you circumnavigated the earth slowly; have you crossed once or many times the international datelines; have you crossed oceans and touched various continents? If not it's your time now to do it; dream about it and it will happen. Locked in your own village, town, or city is great but you must understand the global age. Think of it this way; fly around the world via internet but when you do it in real life the first thing you will notice is that the world never sleeps. There is a constant sunrise somewhere taking place right this very second. Once you completely understand this deeply, all becomes very easy.

The world never sleeps, humans do. The global operations of large or small organizations also never sleep. This 24x7x365 world, with it's around the clock operations provide unlimited accessibility, and it is the place to build. Tapping into the special organizational structuring and response skills is where intelligent planning is required. Remember, this does not mean that the entire staff are sleeplessly working around the clock; not at all, here the organization is structured in such a way that it is actively alive and engaging in professional responsive mode around-the-clock, seven days a week throughout the year. Building an idea, and expanding it or creating an organization on that principle is a remarkable achievement for our modern times.

Once again, massive charting and details of operation against desired overseas markets and their times zones is one of the answers to global age expansion. Assemble a dozen team members anywhere in the world and 25% would be more than happy for the night shift or flexi hours. Imagine a group of 100 or a thousand. All staff discussing new options in order to engage live with overseas markets are and exploring various native language issues. Because of immigration, western nations have large groups of trained bilingual and trilingual people who are ready and able to function with these language issues. In Toronto alone, a team of 100 will easily have over 50 languages spoken amongst them. Now the organization just needs to start creating new timelines, new staff matching and HR issues. Reward and bonuses will need to change. The latest and almost free technologies will make the jobs, connectivity and recordkeeping easy for all. After a few months of struggle, an operation will get surprising results and become global age friendly. Once the process is understood completely, an organization will find it is constantly opening brand-new territories. Once again, it's all about unlearning and rewinding the office clock. Advanced thinking will now be unlearning the use if any of office desks, etc.

Refinements and execution models to build new ideas

Sleep as much as you like, as long you realize that the world never sleeps. Now create an organization that's live and active around the clock all year long. This world never stops; it never shuts down. You have already doubled your reach by figuring ways to eliminate the 9-5 Monday to Friday model, summer and winter holidays, all the other holidays just by respecting the Fact that the world is alive. You too are a living body and an alive organization. The implementation and deployments may take weeks to months, but it can be done. So, what's 24x7x365 world of commerce, we need more understanding.

The Seven dwarfisms

Fact: The world economy is passing through the eye of the needle and in most nations appears barren or at a complete standstill. The global mind-share is seeking bold, clear and honest answers. The global age won't wait for any nation nor will it all allow for the status quo. Major world events are unfolding as you read and brand-new global shifts are upon us.

The Seven Dwarfisms; no matter how insignificantly small or irrelevant they may appear, in Fact, they are the most powerful and freely available global grassroots movements ever faced by the world; they are game changers helping other game changers; it makes no difference who accepts or denies them, it makes no difference who wins or who loses in coming elections. It makes no difference which economy or what country is in the lead, the Fact remains that a powerful global age has already arrived and only those who are part of it are extremely aware of its hy-per-acceleration and positive progress. While for the rest, the spectators, it matters not what they think or do. It's clearly distinct now; the winners and losers of the new global enterprise games will line up in their respec-tive queues. Cavemen were shown no mercy and were forced to accept the wheel. Savvy leaders will move forward and the naysayers will wait until they are forced to change.

Self-Mastery: The following Dwarfisms are the hidden powers that al-low us to freely dive deep and seek out 'self-mastery' because there is no other help along the way. These are the advanced topics and complex challenges of the day.

Lateralization: Is the art of mental compartmentalization sometimes knowing the difference between 'hard asset centricity' and 'soft power asset management'. The questions become, why all over the world, are current factories and plants often so stuck on 'hard asset centricity,' and demonstrate their fears of 'soft power asset management,' progress is about understanding of the difference and bold and open dialogue. The world of commerce is a sophisticated war of innovative excellence and those who are well trained, armored gladiators have the chance for domi-nance while the rest are spectators in the crowd. The global age is moving forward leaving a dust storm of broken and disconnected ideas. Practice the art of differentiation.

Virtualization: Today all you need is high quality VR Goggles. You could be standing on a trading floor of a commodity exchange or on a bull run; now imagine doing all of these events on the same day. Some of us think this is Cyber heaven, while others defiantly think it is cyber hell? When you think of social media, are you in a real social-media-heaven or the an-ti-social-purgatory? The world's next biggest thing since the iPhone is the VR Goggles and Headsets which open yet a brand-new universe. You can travel and walk around the world, climb every mountain while in your bed. You can meet people and attend events that seemed impossible yesterday. You can interact in close real living color encounters with 100 million en-trepreneurs of the world and explore a new universe of brand new billion business opportunities. This will boost commerce like a rocket. Start incorporating this as a special finishing tool for your enterprise.

Trillionization: Unlimited printing of money has peaked. Once society is becoming immune to the trivialization of the trillionization of national debts, and the sound of the term trillion will become sweet music to the ears and a comforting pillow for the citizen's consciousness to sleep on. Who will care how many dozens of trillions are wasted as new debt as long as it rhymes with some illusionary hip hop beat? Success will come when we understand the subject deeply; become good at creating grassroots prosperity to activate an economy with clear vision and brave enough to implement that vision. Debate and differentiate between creating mountains of fake currency or train armies of real entrepreneurs.

Domainization: Is the ownership of a global name identity with a totally undisputed ownership status. A serious business without a solid and exclusive global name ownership is like a dull joke in search of laughter. Only less than 1% enterprises have exclusive ownerships; the remaining 99% of names of big enterprises are each shared with 10 to 10,000 others 'sound-alike or look-alike' names. The most critical issue is to get 'respectable global mindshare' and cultivate globally workable names with the right meaning and association. This is not an easy task. Only well balanced and truly protected name holders will be allowed to play the superior games on global commerce plat forms. Take the time to deeply study how to build a single exclusive global name identity ownership and follow that goal with the highest standards. Image supremacy of any kind is dependent on exclusive universal name identity. The rest is just noise and wasted advertising.

Googlelization: Secures the keys to your free globally connected office. Google has given everyone on the planet the world's largest office for free. This extraordinary platform only needs a smart occupant. It's time to become a Google expert and find all the possible options to build strategies around its access and services. Set up your global office today. Think deeply, act wisely, and grab the keys; enter boldly and do not lock yourself out of the office.

Chapter Thirteen

Innovative excellence is a perpetual exercise

Strategy Six: Alpha dreamers

Definition: The five billion connected dreamers who will change the world.

Usage: Understanding the rise of alpha dreamers as a new world opens.

Symptoms: lack of Intellectualization of the organization on deep and precise understanding of the customers at large; new alliances; new funding; lack of quality contents; right language; better and smarter management.

Ideas-expansion in alpha dreamer friendly world

Should we do nothing to improve our future? If you are connected to the knowledge plug, the world of internet is in your hands. If you are global age friendly, you are open to local, national and global ideas. You are an alpha dreamer of sorts, dreaming for a better future and growing ideas for better grassroots prosperity.

With five billion Alpha dreamers and growing the Alpha dreamers will form the largest and more powerful voice ever.

It's the connectivity global access that makes them more informed and better acquainted with our national and global affairs. You are one of them.

How to build and spread ideas, concepts, and transform organizations require systematic approaches. As we approach 2020, connecting and becoming accessible to five billion well connected individuals from around the globe are the latest challenges of smart marketing communication and art of achieving image supremacy with unique identity in the market place. The Alpha dreamers are ready to move forward, be they big and small, young and old, slim and fat, male and female, rich or poor, novice and experts, they are all connected with immense understanding of the global landscape, and they are eager to learn and expand their horizons. This is the largest assembly ever in the history of civilization; it carries a mindshare larger than any power of any superpower nation, and it has the accumulated GDP that represents almost the entire world. This is a sleeping giant and the sooner we learn, understand and most importantly, make use of this collective energy, the sooner we will build unheard of success. It is time to dig deep within ourselves and learn to engage and dance in a world where dreaming becomes a common dominator. This is one of the most critical challenges of global age positioning. The ultimate mandate is to dream a better future.

Dreams lay the foundations for future realities

Rise of the alpha dreamers

Alpha dreamers are the five billion connected people of the world increasing in numbers by the second, advancing their knowledge by the day and become globally aware by the month…they are becoming capable of dreaming a better future.

Alpha dreamers can easily recognize this new global age. They are connected and hard-wired to real life, and they are soft-wired to Technocalamity. They think differently because their exposure is global, they speak a different language, because they are interested in global issues, act distinctively different because they love technology, now a rising steadily, quietly they change the world. They can easily isolate truth, eliminate junk overload and respond to real information. Because they are invisible, the media has failed to identify this hidden new demographic. Nevertheless, as a new global mind-share, their harmonious presence and superior thinking moves them toward prolonged peaceful living and global sustainability issues keeps infusing them with new energies. They are the frontline inquisitors who are exploring the hidden powers of mankind; yet they fully appreciate the human frailty and the mystery of its origin. They have collaboration built into their genes. They are blind to skin colors and deaf to dogmas; they are comfortable with global age thinking and execution. They are continually seeding for worldwide prosperity and they represent the new consciousness of mankind. Their silence is the next thunder.

Let's explore the gradual arrival of this new 'Global Age' and how Alpha dreamers erupted gradually to become the unlimited thinkers of today.

The internet was the main reason for the emerging of the Alpha dreamers; they were born with it and additional technologies and smart mobile devices have given them unmatchable power; In addition, their number are growing with mammoth proportions.

Whatever your ideas, you must look at this as key force; this population will grow further. They will communicate and bounce like no other section of our previous classes or civilizations did, they could interact and engage in a round the clock 24x7x365 rhythm, construct new ideas and new progress.

Create a maze of countries, select contact points and go global, study maps and international news by markets and regions.

Assign key people on key markets and allocate global mandates.

Think, eat, sleep, global.... it's the only way.

The seeding of worldwide prosperity demands the elimination of white-collar thinking. This new global age thinking, with its wisdom and execution, will steadily wipe out last century white collar thinking. The towers of bureaucracies with its cascading incompetency camouflaged with built-in corruption will collapse. Such passé age skill will be replaced by instant and simple black and white checks and balances, bottom-line results, and honest tabulations. It will be surrounded by automation and robotics pushing rapid fire technologies, and it will be driven by the hyper-speed global age execution. There is just no escape.

Cavemen were shown no mercy

Cavemen were shown no mercy but forced to accept the wheel. What's going on? The world is moving ahead at its own special speed. It is producing, consuming, charging and dancing and this tempo will not slow down for anyone. As these changes occur, the highly agenda centric doom and gloom mind numbing media blasts only serve the divisive dog-whistling political leaders. Out there, the real world is very different and for every one bad thing happening, there are thousands of better events occurring with astounding options. There are tadpole's and bird's eye views. The sky is not falling and this new global age living is primarily for global age friendly players. Living in this global age demands new knowledge and new thinking.

The Alpha dreamers; they are like the new universal citizens.

They are bold because they are not afraid of global age and Technocalamity; they are confident because they know more about smart deployment of resources than their local government administrators or politicians; they are entrepreneurial and know about better job creation with massive prosperity to solve social problems; they are getting seriously organized because they have lost faith in those once established institutions that are now drowning in incompetency or corruption. Most importantly Alpha dreamers are neither afraid to change and push their own personal transformation into superior performance nor are they afraid of breaking the many old rigid rules, ways of thinking or procedures around them. They are getting ready to openly lead the next prosperity revolution. They are the first ever largest and well-connected group in the history of mankind.

Fact: A new dawn emerges towards 2020. Towers of paper-based-bureaucracies ruled the world and later were wiped out in the post-software transition era. They shrank into a CD and are now left in drawers of empty offices. Now Block Chain technology of crypto-currencies and time-stamped data base systems will eliminate and replace most needs of financial, legal, medical and other professional expertise in this massive push-button automation. This will be the biggest revolution since the start of the Internet. It will impact billions of professionals.

Fact: The comfortable cultures of the past, for example the rotary phones, room size computers and floors of filing cabinets era; new and innovative changes were fiercely resisted. History will show that most technological advancements were met with opposition.

Question: Some smart nations are now thinking of letting one million entrepreneurs land within the country under special concessions, taxations, visas and immigration in order to create local prosperity and revolutionize massive job creation, while many dumb countries are building walls. Some 100 million entrepreneurs are mobile around the world looking for fertilized options and a far better quality of life. Which nation has the foresight, which country the organizational infrastructures and which leadership has the guts?

How far is the horizon; when will the sun rise and what will happen at high-noon?

Once, at the invent of electricity, coming out of the darkness into light was the biggest challenge facing the world: As we move forward in time, it becomes obvious that once again it's not the invented things that make the differences; rather it is the deeper thinking and the use of advanced skills that will push us ahead. For example, the discovery of electricity was not the all-important issue. We had to come to grips emotionally and physically to the drastic lifestyle changes that this discovery made to our lives. Continuous life style adjustments and deployment of that invention drove us to a massive transformation. It was not just a light switch but rather coming out of the darkness into light was the main challenge. This is also the case now as we to come out of our metal cubes and boxes and launch into open cyber connected wide-open global age spaces. We must not be scared like house trained kittens and too scared to step into the front yards. We are at the cusp of overly invented ideas which seriously lack deployments while we are emotionally afraid to let go of our heavy filing cabinets and squared cubicles and afraid of boundary-less living.

Refinements and execution models to build new ideas

Study the world map closely, observe how many nations are advancing via connectivity and interexchange of ideas, place yourself, your ideas and your vision in the center. Start all over. Soon you will start seeing things, new options, open few contacts here and there and more contacts. Never give up, the connected five billion are also looking for you. This is boundaryless, an infinite market, ready to absorb great new ideas.

The plugged society

The Crown: To crown our civilization, the internet surpasses all the other earth-shattering advances of the last 2000 years, from firecrackers to a-bombs, steam to stealth flying wings or abacus to tablet. Nothing comes even close to the power and value of what society recently invented and what its summative functionality that is referred worldwide as the internet.

It's most powerful in the right hands and can bring governments and super powers to their knees

144

It's most beneficial to the entire global populations and it provides economic growth.

It's easy to use, free, global and always alive, constantly growing, unstoppable and omnipresent.

It's the ultimate assembly of 'knowledge' and ever instantly delivered in usable form by Homo-erectus.

As a direct beneficiary of this, the greatest gift from America to the world, we are now, decades later, ushering in a brand-new era. On the other hand, China and India who are seeking independence from America may have their own Internets in coming years. This split will make global shock waves on web traffic and also point to market segmentation and threaten the global universality of the digital access. Domain names will flip and morph into new systems and massive disruptions will occur. Cyber-branding will be re-invented and the world of commerce will become a totally different and confusing place.

Global Age Pragmatism: Plugged Society is neither for the highly technologically literate nor the artificially intelligence driven masses of people. It is rather like a simple driver of a high-speed self-driven car commuting to work, yet more advanced than ever in the history of civilization on pragmatic knowledge and deeper understanding of humanistic needs with survival and concerns for creating grassroots prosperity. The plugged society will have more real knowledge than the old bureaucratic masters. This is where the previous societies, over the last 100 years due to lack of free and timely global access to facts resulted in failures. Being Knowledge plugged with pragmatism is the light in the darkness.

The Internet of Things; There is no such thing as the 'internet' with 'things'. When did we drop our smart phones inside our toasters? When was the last time we strapped a banana to our mobile phone? The Internet of Things is an old-style advertising agency charade branding nomenclature that is now outdated. Things have changed big time in last few years. The Internet with hundreds of points of connectivity is now advancing into just like an omnipresent single "knowledge plug" basically for billions to plug it to get instant access to universal knowledge.

Today, it's not that important how much education we have. What is important is how smartly we are plugged into this universal knowledge. Here are the timely tests of new superior level smartness for players claiming to have innovative economic growth and entrepreneurial excellence.

Test:

How well adjusted and exposed are we in this knowledge-plugged society?

How and what do we know about how to deploy the power of knowledge plug today?

How many models of value creation and prosperity generation can we articulate?

How can we demonstrate our global age leadership qualities during this metamorphosis?

Chapter Fourteen

Hallucination is a natural cause, but real vision is a luxurious gift

Strategy Seven: Quadrability formation

Definition: mastery of four-dimensional thinking styles and multidirectional advancements.

Usage: how to create four times the productivity, four times the performance and four times the profitability.

Symptoms: Standstill no-action mode; Silence and do not rock the boat mentality; Silos and disconnections of all complex issues; critical need for interactive and bold dialogue to demonstrate consensus, while improving multidimensional thinking and execution

Manage and expand in four dimensions.

Should we avoid any additional complex thinking models?

The Quadrability Management Style and Thinking: During the last century you needed a stuffed leather recliner chair, a massive oak desk in a huge office to be a boss. A decade ago, a corner office was reserved for the boss and during the last few years just a cubicle was enough. Today, you need nothing. No massive offices, decorum, or filing cabinets. Nothing is required except your brain powers and some shared space. Either you have the skills or you don't. One-single-hour in a high-speed global age modern office is enough to disqualify a well experienced and senior executive person if they lack an understanding of technology, e-commerce and the latest global age enterprise expertise. So, do not get rejected. In this empty office-less-office space, your mind is all that is needed. Harnessing the powers and unlearning and relearning of this miracle organ of the universe called mind is where the future corporate battles will be fought. Creating sophisticated thinking, articulating and comprehending global age skills in multiple dimensions with simultaneous thinking and execution like a maestro conducting a symphony is the art. You have it all and all this requires decisions, discipline and action, and the rest becomes easy.

Quadrability Management Learnings: How to adopt new style of management to fit the global age and Alpha dreamers. The Quadrotectonic Shifts and multi-dimensional thinking. The formation and thinking for building unheard of success: this new global age demands and Quadrability management delivers your idea development and organizational structure so that you can operate, function and execute all the steps in four dimensions simultaneously and in synchronicity with all the other aspects of the organization. This is accomplished with fascinating ease. This new thinking requires you to fully grasp and accept the new landscapes, the new realities and to practice the processes until they become a normal part of how you live and function. With practice you will operate in four dimensions, creating four times the productivity and four times the profit. You will then be continually building prosperity and not just surviving.

Four-dimensional thinking

Make a list of all the pending issues for next 100 days, start training your mind to see them being executed simultaneously as a movie set where a major production is underway. Can you be just an actor on stage to read your line or can you be the Director of the movie who has responsibility to several dozen other aspect in simulations execution around the lines an actor is reading. Watch your favorite movie but not as viewer rather place yourself behind the camera as a Director and now try to watch the entire movie from his vantage point. You will be shocked. This is all your mind and you and how you train it. These are special skills you can also take advanced level training and courses to become good at.

Mental demands beyond 2020

No matter what happens, a force of gravity of our human advancements will issue new decrees. Beyond 2020 you will be asked to demonstrate your cognitive flexibility at every major step. Your mental performance will have a direct impact on your judgment at high-speed decision making. Emotional stability and well-trained thinking will also help in such situations and showcase your intelligence as all this will be measured against how your decisions fit into the local-global market place, performance, productivity and profitability. Your fine art of being able to clearly differentiate from the uncontrolled and casual creative after thoughts against highly structured and organized creativity managed by critical thinking and complex problem solving will eventually provide you with superior performance. Creativity is a spark of genius, over creativity can cause fire and damage. All ideas can be good to explore but most ideas end up being useless for lack of structure and execution. Understanding the critical difference right at the starting point showcases deeper understanding and global age thinking. Self-learning and relearning will foster new progress. No one can help you here, only your mind and how it allows you to tango with your daily grinds and still advance steadily into deeper and more analytical canyons. Only your mind will allow you to grow. Silence of surrounding is a start; silence of mind is the early development and cognition of having such controls is a sign of being on the right trajectory.

How ready are you to prove that your vision and your ideas are far more valuable and superior in original thinking over your opposing teams who are armed with fearful facts, accounting numbers and prohibitive budgets? The last 1000 earth shattering global inventions were not approved by accountants and fearful administrations. But this must not keep you from laying out your own original game plan. Entrepreneurial leadership is all about marching ahead where others fear to tread. Do not act without deep thinking and do not think new ideas without fine details of execution. Millions of the heavily invested innovations of today are still rolled up as dead sea scrolls filed away and forgotten, missing development, all due to lack of entrepreneurial execution and deployments. Ideas without executions are useless.

Without suffering there is no room to grow new ideas; in darkness comes vision, in chaos creativity. Accidental experiences can create sometimes failures to become lessons and successes to become advancements. The mind is capable of tackling all issues. Allow it to take charge. Work in harmony and educate the mind; educate the heart and educate the body. This is how you create your own future.

The advanced stage will help you move out from the darkness, strengthen the weakness, mend the broken and reenergize your vitality from top to bottom. Create your own goals and desires, follow your own methodologies and learn the art of comfortably sacrificing, identifying the irrelevant distractions in your way, don't allow them to prevent you from reaching your goal, move forward and plan a route to reach your ultimate destination.

In the global age commerce, quadrability formation, the thinking and executing in four-dimensional thinking, quadrupling productivity, performance and profitability is a new way.

The healing of incompetence

When life-long-learning advancement issues are raised, proof may be required if our minds are capable of deciphering truth from fakery.

There is nothing wrong with incompetency; it is a serious liability when hidden that becomes a gift when discovered and understood. Identified, isolated and readjusted. In-competencies at times have merits. Old experiences at times have great values. The real dangers are the traditional political correctness and corporate decorum that hides all and prolong the agony and let poor performances become standards.

The entrepreneurial mind is constantly cognizant of one's incompetency, but will still toy with it while taking big and small risks. It can intertwine failures into powerful ropes. The academic and bureaucratic mind is more dependent on business plans, case studies and endorsement of peers, and it is terribly frightened of failures and therefore freezes when called to actions away from the fermentation of prolonged incompetency. Bureaucratic seniority is the proof of incompetency. Check around for proof. Anyone on the economic development front who is doing exactly what they did few years ago is already deemed incompetent.

This is a new world. Clinical psychology and related neuroscience disciplines of the world have yet to tackle such specific corporate performance issues because they too come from the same academic molds. The world of mental performance measurements must answer to the role of overflow of free technologies or hide in their own comfort box of bureaucratic malfunction.

To entrepreneurs all this psychological and mental measurement mumbo jumbo craft is crazy to start with. However extreme entrepreneurialism itself is very crazy. Only crazy people sleeping on air-filled mattresses created Airbnb. Their craziness, initially joked at, resulted in acquiring the world's highest market evaluation in the hospitality industry, while the old genuine wisdom of the carriage trade hotelier remained stuffed within their monolithically grand hotels. There are millions of such examples that became local or global legends and most came from incompetent starts. Incompetency must come on the forefront and juxtaposed with global age talents to create a new dimension and new standard of performance.

We must know if we are a real trained jumbo pilot and fit for the cockpit or just a frequent flyer pretending to be a pilot. Now we know why the economical agendas come crashing down and why the smoke of corporate fiascos linger. Why nations are failing, why organizations are stuck? Why the screams for profitability? Why the chaos? Why the fog? Around the world, the fake leaderships, miss-match job-titles on business cards and politically corrected cover-ups of in-competencies prohibiting healing and relearning.

Fact: Top 100 earth shattering business models were developed by people without any formal training and by those who did not care if their special competence failed or had grand results.

Fact: It's the deeper study of physical and mental limitations that isolates hidden powers and ensures gold medal victories in the Olympics.

Fact: Every smart leader today will eventually become incompetent during the next decade unless a regimented program to continuously improve performance is followed.

When skyscrapers arrived, people learned how to push elevator buttons. Now there are 100 new buttons in need of pushing or we will end up on wrong floors.

Creeping slowly into incompetency is a very normal process; great abnormal leaders are always cognizant and constantly thinking in this reality. Now those with great mastery from the past, but who deny changing times, are severely incompetent and they are a liability to the organizations of today. The obvious symptoms are their silence and rejection of any bold open dialogue on innovative excellence, change, advancement and global age affairs and Technocalamity.

Discover, identify and isolate incompetency and start the healing process or lose all the other hidden talents. Here is a test of smartness for key players claiming to be the savior of innovative growth and entrepreneurial excellence.

Tango Incompetencia

Despite all skills, each single executive, at some point becomes outdated, sooner or later. This happens every decade but now at hyper-accelerated pace. Turn your "lingering incompetency" into your tango dance partner and teach them new steps; it is time to relearn to stay on the dance floor, enjoy the spotlight rather than tripping all over or finding yourself outside the dance hall all together.

Five signs of being outdated.

You have stopped debating your new ideas and have stopped listening to new ideas of others.

You have difficulty grasping the contents in meeting and do not question where these contents might go.

You feel others are watching you sideways and you are fearful of what that may mean.

You feel overly stressed for no reason and cannot see ways to eliminate that stress.

You become increasingly very busy with little or no progress

Five methods will make you a dancing star

Eliminate 50% of your work, relax and the sky will not fall. Your work may be already too outdated anyway. Start a deep-thinking process to improve your craft and rediscover your new core competencies. Start a relearning process that will lead to a new point of view; do not compete with technology but support it. Mastery is good but sometime requires you to become a "master of ceremonies on collaborative synthesizes; lead the dance and lead the party. Start a daily challenging discussion; lead in meetings; start entrepreneurial ways of thinking and doing things

Dance all the time; Business is a dance, collaborative synthesizim is a dance party, just relearn the steps and begin moving across the floor with the ease and grace of a pro. Hear and feel the beauty of Tango Incompetencia

Can you tackle a bigger challenge and mobilize a large-scale program to uplift midsize economy? Can you open and engage a Cabinet Level meeting with your local, regional, or national leadership and articulate on how to expand markets, quadruple exports and create sophisticated digital platforms to connect to the global age world. All blueprints, all mastery and unlearning and relearning is available in a most pragmatic way, but are you and your team ready for such challenges.

Test:

How comfortable are we with our own level of competencies?

How can we showcase our hidden and untapped talents?

How much are we willing to openly discuss and debate?

How fearless are we to discover that our greatest rewards in the future maybe hidden in these tough processes?

Chapter Fifteen

Enter first whenever a new door opens and worry later

Strategy Eight: The global age

Definitions: The global age is a post e-commerce cultural and entrepreneurial shift.

Usage: acquiring trend-hunting mastery, when growth is absent; understanding global age and open new markets.

Symptoms: Management has little or no ideas on the top trends forcing the industry; lack of superiority of knowledge, decision making and execution; lack of understanding of the global age, and lack of thought leadership on market differentiation

Acquiring trend-hunting mastery

Should we only live on a day-to-day business planning model? Mastery is necessarily not abundance of knowledge; mastery is knowing which button to push for that knowledge.

Leadership is moving forward; leadership is going in the right direction and advanced knowledge is what leaders are very good at, because they are years and decades ahead on trends and future. Become such a leader.

The world is moving really fast. The question becomes in what direction is it moving and if that specific direction is where your idea is headed. If not, you must evaluate the idea with logic and advance level reasoning backed by global age skills. You must be able to justify your reasoning in light of global age needs. Amateurish whims will kill the idea forever. Furthermore, based on the direction and the blowing winds, know what type of structure will it hold on its own as it is blast from these winds. Determine if you are building a single dwelling or a world-class skyscraper. Here smartness and intelligence are openly displayed with clear reasoning and concentration on upcoming trends and forecasts so one could stay ahead of the curve. Trends that alter our daily lives invisibly suddenly bring us closer to a fast-moving future. Lack of global age knowledge will keep your idea in the dark and your organization in abyss. This is when change must NOT appear like shockwaves, but rather an expected visitor. Read the winds and constantly change with the tic-toc of the clock, otherwise sudden storm will hit you very hard.

Now even in the smallest towns and villages of the world given the smart technology access mid-size companies reach and their global power that was once reserved for only Fortune 100 enterprises. Today it's less about funding and more about execution; less about MBA certification and more about entrepreneurialism and less about old hard work and more about smart work.

Major global advancing cycles are already imbedded in mankind's transformational psyche, are now finally awake, altering thinking and perceptions that will manifest themselves into massive behavioral changes.

This global realignment of human at this scale has never ever happened before.

The Re-definitions of Work: The thousand-year old mindsets of earning models and job structuring will evaporate. Routines and annual distribution of time, with defined expected productivity based on the Julian Calendar that now impacts our daily, weekly, monthly and yearly regimented social and work fabric and culture will fade into the past.

What is work and who does what and what will be determined by algorithms? The elimination of white-collar expertise will morph towards entrepreneurialism and only very smart work will be left for very smart workers, eliminating the 9-5 rat races that so drastically impact daily lives. New living styles and new intellectualism are emerging. How many nations are equipped and open to having the majority of their citizenry adopt such dramatic changes?

When office cubicles start leaving buildings, downtowns and corporate hierarchies will morph, impacting economies with cities redefining their purpose and suburbia begins to bloom even more brightly. New styles of consumerism and distribution of products will occur. The confused future of 10,000 cities will start bouncing amidst super-smart living.

In a smart thinking world, being busy will become a sign of being too old fashioned and be replaced with free-flow thinking where we will dive deep into global age expansion issues. Smart machines will do smart work; mankind will think of ways to mass deploy smart technologies and stay ahead of the curves. The global bureaucracies will no longer be filled by smart people, but rather by smart technology and robotic solutions.

Globally speaking, "entrepreneurialism" is always diverse and tolerant; it is the present political types of leadership that's not broadminded. Making national mobilization of entrepreneurialism as a major, open, national mandate, a better world would emerge as nations would be more occupied with expanding fair trading and grassroots prosperity.

The global-age mastery

The master idea will be when global masses realize that what's good enough for everyone in the world will automatically become good enough for themselves too. Therefore, solving issues globally, no matter how large or small they will eventually in the long run create better local harmony and local prosperity for all. The collective mind, the collective conscious, the new global age thinking sound simple but they are extremely hard to achieve. The secrets of the global age wisdom are hidden within the five billion online connected people called "Alpha dreamers", the new global age thinkers of the world, the new dream weavers of mankind who with their new wisdom will look out for humanity at large.

When global populous simultaneously start interacting with each other in real time

When global public consciousness surpasses all other forces and starts taking its own new shape

When the global pulse of hyper activity becomes simultaneously unstoppable with new methodologies

When global populous recognizes global problems and starts seeking globally workable answers

When global mindshare starts connecting in order to stop the abuse of global issues.

When global mindshare starts placing global issues above their own national issues

When global populace starts calling themselves as global citizens

When global populace starts getting comfortable recognizing our times as the global age

Why discovering and understanding of approaching trends well in advance is so critically necessary for better navigation in our global age?

Builders of ideas must become trained readers of global age trends as the performance of their ideas will be determined by this unique level of literacy and how they navigate their progress forward, while novices will be found in a state of shock and frozen forms. Here Global Age understanding is defined as a means to kindle trend-hunting skills

Dreams always lay the foundations for building new realities.

Without dreaming there is nothing but fear, insecurities and panic. Alpha dreamers are well armed, each with super connectivity devices of some kind, internet savvy, and with the capability to mobilize intuitive wisdom in order to survive. World control and influences are increasingly not in the hands of a small percentage of power brokers but in the minds of new tidal waves of global age masses. The most obvious proof of this is hidden in the endless lingering and bickering amongst power brokers over their own decisions and the visible incapability of once powerful and fast action super-mighty government bodies.

We are at the dawn of the biggest and largest formation of global mindshare ever. This awakening of global consciousness, increasingly synchronized on mankind issues take priority, where last millennia societies phenomenally flourished, while totally oblivious or concerned about others or the rest of the globe. Now it's the pulsating the globe, audible to Alpha dreamers. The loud and powerful stentorian call will be heard. The global mind share will strive to survive the destructive ideologies and transform them for the betterment of humanity. The beast within will be tamed by the rapid-fire access to truth and 'real' global information. Localized dogmas will slowly die out.

Creating Common Sense; are you ready for some testing?

Mankind is hardwired to understand darkness but when brightly lit chandeliers start creating even more darkness, only common sense will be able to find the way out. Mind can find ways in darkness; humans eventually can differentiate between reality and invented fakery.

A new revolution of common sense rises worldwide. The question is, how does this help builders. Elimination of political correctness has now liberated masses all over the world to start speaking. Plain talk starts; bold common-sense questioning starts and new global mindshare emerges. The truth finally starts unfolding.

The decades of fooling all the people all of the times are almost over.

Smartness: defined as simple global age awareness and responses to commonly visible realities on the ground; all this is more about informed deployment of common sense. It is, however, not to be confused with IQ Tests, the super twisted and moronic 100 years old notion of the period labeled as IQ, the intelligent quotient designed to measure and differentiate smart or idiotic responses of monkeys to human savants. IQ was the Holy Grail of human resource management of the West during last part of last century. Not any longer.

Success of any global dialogue is hidden in its extreme simplicity; the simple words, the thoughts and in the simple sequence with simple logic.

Survival of the fittest was needed during the horse and buggy days. Today's survival of the mind to see the truth is in order. Mental and intellectual stamina based on wisdom and not brute force is where the difference lies.

Health is always wealth, but wealth is not just muscle building, rather mental endurance and elasticity to change and adopt and allowing common sense to direct it. Today, good sense and mental gymnastics is the order of the day, because when failures lead to more failures, common sense becomes the pilot. It works all by itself even in darkness.

The print society

Some 120 years ago, *"during the 1900s and the Print Society, when printed words were power, literacy was required and information was restricted to the educated elite. Since that time during every couple of decades, new*

transformational metamorphisms altered economic lifestyle and human be-
haviors; The Radio Society, brought music and free information on air. The
TV Society brought color and personalities and commercialization. The Tele-
com Society, eliminated distance and global standards; the Computer Society
miniaturization and brought the world to the desk, The Cyber Society created
instant living and placed the world in our pockets." (Sunrise Day One, Year
2000, by Naseem Javed - Originally published by Communication World,
IABC December 1995)

Right now, we are the Plugged Society. We are connected to a single
universal knowledge plug. More informed with far more knowledge and
live transactional data than ever in the history of civilization.

During the Print Society by the time worldly knowledge was acquired it
took a life time and the person was almost on the death bed by the time
knowledge was accumulated. Today in the Plugged Society, a ten years
old kid has thousands of times more access to knowledge in immediate
useable formats. Despite lacking the experience, understanding of deployment, the young person possesses the immense depth or awareness
or richness of the provided knowledge all to enable better decision making at much earlier stages. This never happened to mankind before.

Will the Millennial suddenly transform themselves from the currently
labeled Lost Generation status to become the most advanced common-
sensical driven society that will liberate all of us from the current fog and
darkness?

Is this how mankind finds its way to survival? Historically, when all the
brilliance and complex strategies behind the big and small wars, it was
only the common sense in the end that led to ordinary thinking and allowed mankind to prevail.

The transition from the Print Society to the TV Society took half a century; today from Telecom to Cyber Society took half of that time. The
Plugged Society with full impact will be here by 2020. As far as occupation is concerned, the people will be forced to think; they will outsmart
the system and invent or innovate something very brand new. Absence of

this caliber of this type of thinking will push people to mundane assignments. Some one billion educated and experienced executives who were the masters of the old systems and procedures will be challenged against common sense and global age entrepreneurial innovative thinking.

Action: Imagine a world where job titles are eliminated. It's no longer how your business card describes you but rather what can you do better than anyone else; it will be about what the enterprise can count on you for performing. The game plan is to nurture and cultivate deeper thinking and replace job description and complex procedures to pure and deeper 'thinking'. Visualize your position as Executive Vice President of Thinking. Prepare to witness the start of bonfires of bureaucracies that will illuminate the sky with lights of prosperity.

Question: will the new world of young and old Alpha dreamers, the first ever young and informed generation, be able to formulate consensus on globally workable solutions. Will they be able to use a deeper understanding of mankind, peace and order and use that understanding to help build a better world?

Government of the people for the people and by people overtime became 'government of the government for and by the government" it's losing its credibility and is searching for new styles and formats. Every organization is in the throngs of these serious and timely challenges.

Breakdown: The future has arrived. Technocalamity has fully landed; transformation has begun and Alpha dreamers are fully aware of this. They are marching ahead and now it's the difference between known and unknown. The new future is hidden between the classroom-smarts and the common-sense global age smart. Time for building and living in the smart age is here; building and thriving in the global age is the essential.

The role of entrepreneurialism

At a junction, when global age nouveau entrepreneurialism is already out there creating few billion micro-solo enterprises, millions of high-quality exporters and thousands of mushy and cute baby 'Ali Babas' are changing the local and global economic landscapes. The new age of 'extreme value creation' and 'extreme image generation' is erupting surrounded by Technocalamity? The real pragmatic entrepreneurs with solid hard-core programs based or real pragmatism will boom. The long histories of incubators and start-ups all over the world have also helped. Unfortunately, they are mostly new Apps-driven groups in search of being the next Hypos, Rhinos and Unicorns type billion-dollar ideas. Evaluations of this type of thinking may face some harsher realities.

No other experiment of human endeavor has been as successful as America. America is the only nation on the planet that can still showcase real world-class examples of revolutionary entrepreneurial thinking and bring about a major change and uplift dreams. Any policy to help this front will produce great results and grassroots happiness within USA and also spread across the world. Many aggressive nations are watching with great interest as American entrepreneurism revival may tango with emerging world ideas.

A great America is also great for the world

Global age execution; without thriving businesses and entrepreneurial gusto, innovation mantras are at best just day dreaming. Entrepreneurs already have magical ideas in need of collaborative attention. It is essential to note that only ideas worthy of investing get funding in the first place. Ideas without details and execution plans are basically useless.

Fact: Innovation events are either very focused on technology issues or academic approaches while deployments is disconnected from today's entrepreneurial challenges and realties. After the events, the 364 remaining days seem to bring about very little progress or worse, nothing happens. How fast can they become perpetual forces?

Fact: The absence of senior level political leadership with bold debates and combative discussions on hard core issues of innovative excellence and achieving global image supremacy is the proof of a serious lack of knowledge. True and real Entrepreneurial components are so visibly absent in the bureaucratic maze. How soon will this change?

Observe the major excuses immediately

No Funds Excuse: The absence of money should not create a vacuum for expansion of Image Supremacy and innovative excellence; it should not lead to the loss of a critical needs for spotlights. The most common mantra in almost every boardroom is the lack of funding. World Bank, The White House or all the banks of the world need money; so, does every single organization. Only those creative entrepreneurial leaderships capable of framing their value propositions and precisely articulate their vision become magnets for new money to move forward. Those frozen in a constant state of excuses wait for a funding miracle to happen. These are the people who get in the way of progress. Just reassign them.

No new Exports Sales Excuse: If our products are good for one city, then they are good for 10,000 cities. If our offerings can already outsmart 100 other competitors then we must also get ready to outsmart additional 1000 more. If we are shipping to one country get ready to ship to 200 more. Do not just read newspapers, read the world maps also. Study every single day; examine the little dots on the maps and realize that they are cities and most many times bigger and brighter than where we are probably located today. These 10,000 dots on the maps are consuming, dancing, thriving and may have no idea about our great inventions and our charming offerings unless we try and knock on their doors. This is to understand global age in real terms. Look very closely and figure it out. Use the hammock, think, imagine, and reflect. Learn and hear the deep humming of collaborations and outbound explorations of global markets.

Too Much Competition Excuse: Too much competition is actually very good; it's a positive sign of the bustling market. Never be afraid of competition, but be very afraid of our own short comings, the kinds, styles and types of handicaps. As this is where super creativity will spark an idea that someday historians may write about. Never be afraid of any external performance or quality issues but please get petrified as you discover hiding your own competencies and   short comings. Open to relearn, open to submerge and demand immediate skills that can be pragmatically deployed and support innovative excellence and the supremacy of entrepreneurialism. Constant analysis and identification of short comings will result in better performance and profitability. This can't wait; it must be done immediately. The global age progress tempos do not allow for slow yearlong reports and case studies.

Test

How skilled is our team on global age execution or are they just corporate-politic-centric?

How clear is our leadership vision or does it require global age re-evaluation?

How can we showcase extreme world-class value offering or is it just a nice flakey idea?

How ready are we to transform overnight or are we satisfied to simply linger into the next decade?

Propagandized nations

Today, proof is required if we are propagandized or an independently smart nation? During the last decade we created bounce of our real-life issues which collided with baked and fake news. This created chaos of propagandized sensationalism resulting in the massive failure of media credibility and exposed solid proofs of the controlled agenda centricities. All of the panic buttons were pushed; the full throttle of baked and barking news was released in all directions, and all was done all over the world. The global populace has now acquired deeper knowledge. The media is getting shutdown. Now media sound bites, all over the world, are being accepted as a sign of misinformation and propaganda. Truth and fakery are being sorted. Shrieking nasality of TV Anchors is getting gentler.

Fact: The more unlimited the information that is spewed, the more chances of creating limited intelligence for the people. Today excessive nonsense and surgically sequenced media information has become a liability. Learn to unlearn and relearn.

Test

How do we demonstrate our freedom from fake propaganda?

How do we deploy knowledge and get mindshare while remaining free from media hype?

How do we prove our smartness and what original sources of information will we use?

How do we gain momentum without media and rebuild our new credible institutions?

Globe age smartness and trend hunting

Can you identify the top trend in your sector with some in-depth knowledge? Can you articulate few trends in your markets with some authority, can you predict some trends in your areas of expertise with commanding knowledge? Study the current affairs of our technologically advanced world. It's all there but only visible to open minded curious observers. Builders of new ideas, new vision and new journeys are all curious observers otherwise they would not be at the post. Just realign your thinking it's natural for you.

Chapter Sixteen

Being an entrepreneur is like dangling on a rope,
trusting the rope, and trusting own capabilities to climb,
no matter the swings, just keep moving upwards

Strategy Nine: Grassroots prosperity

Definition: How to help local-national-global landscape at the grassroots level.

Usage: Social responsibility to create local grassroots prosperity,

Symptoms: Lack of social responsibility and knowledge on how to mobilize local or regional programs to help the community grow; lack of contents to make Cabinet level presentations and stand up as a leader

Idea fertilization; creating grass roots prosperity umbrella for the enterprise and the rise of entrepreneurial mind

The entire grassroots prosperity advancements of the world, since the times of caves, were all delivered by the entrepreneurial minds. It was the doing of entrepreneurial growth that created our modern times. Not to be confused with high-level money-making schemes to strip the public of any benefits.

Should we only be happy with our own prosperity and not care about others?

Entrepreneurs do not only dream of stacks of gold bars in their safes, they dream of being responsible for delivering earth shattering ideas for the benefit of mankind. They are dramatically different because they take personal responsibility for the advancement of their workers. If they are not thinking like this then they are not entrepreneurs they are the market wolves, creating fake economies and hedging on fake prosperity.

Grassroots Prosperity is a natural gift of human toil. Integrity is already a hardwired superior quality of mankind. When fakery becomes the dominant, truth becomes its prime enemy and this is where mankind starts to slip on grassroots prosperity performance and disproportionate rewards start creating fake economies.

In one hour of research on the internet you will learn how leading economies are collapsing and only servicing the very top. You will also see a billion new and old entrepreneurs and their independent and un-supported efforts falling on deaf ears of the national leadership who are already mandated and in charge of creating grassroots prosperity. Now you have two options, survive or build; stand up with your inno-vative ideas and create entrepreneurial moves and chase your dreams. With this in place the rest becomes easy.

Your ideas can create grassroots prosperity, sustainable growth, and serve the society at large. Difficult questions must be answered and demand-ing deep and thoughtful answers will make your ideas stand out from crazy get rich quick money-making schemes. Now, Advanced thinking of grassroots prosperity.

Economical metamorphism

No matter what, ideas, dreams and innovative ventures are almost use-less without understanding grassroots prosperity. We must demonstrate modern-day hunter/gatherer skills in a refined, wise and more efficient ways. We must justify our existence; we must beg forgiveness for being cruel to nature and mankind. We must kneel to our minuscule existence as our earth hurled like a dust particle in a storm of galaxies takes us to unknown passages. We must strive for grassroots property; we must lead, follow or get out of the way

All over the world, mega organization, institutions and government administrations are immersed in tackling the unsolved mysteries of economic chaos. It is time to come to the realization that the world has already moved on and will no longer wait for any power. The problems are now almost incurable and it's time for a complete economical metamorphism.

The global-age has now morphed the world; the metamorphosis has now advanced, so study very deeply but from a 'butterfly's vantage point' and not from a caterpillar's disposition. Allow your mind to travel to where your hidden mental powers transform into new ideas, spread wings and show colors while flying. As staying trapped at your current situations is where the caterpillar is that only relies on crawling.

Currently we have entered in a dark tunnel of confusion; on the other side a new global age economical metamorphosis will take place. This unstoppable and natural course of human development is the same as when the impact of Gutenberg's printing press changed the world. It took a century and now the Internet and Social media took less than half of that time. Every process with which we interact and every lifestyle altering advantage we create will be impacted; positively yes, but most importantly it will be based on our vantage point. While we wait, here are the monster collisions we can anticipate. Now with billions of UBER-rides around the world, next will be personal self-driven cars; imagine hundreds of UBER cars available online on demand in our 'personalized transportation systems', eliminating car ownership and maintenance. These types of on demand door to door service programs are creating shock waves in mobile consumption. Now this is moving to private jets and yachts. Need to drive and its compulsive importance will become irrelevant. The saving of energy will place the personal car population back to the styles of 1950s. Oil is losing its importance. The emerging and population rich nations will deploy technology over ownership of multiple cars and endless driving. Amazing transformation with new opportunities. Unlearn being a driver on a seat relearn sitting in a mobile self-driven office.

Beneficiaries: New global age thinkers and practitioners; a car becomes a service.

Enemies: The oil-addicted mentality and the enforced auto manufacturing bases from the last century.

Adjustments: The imagine of being limo driven all the time and never having to pump gas.

Alternate Workspace: 9-5 model of office is dying fast. The office-less offices, exotic shared spaces, where result driven high-performance smart skills will simply fly out, free of cubicle and in their own comfort zone. There will be no commuting-jams, no elevators, or water-coolers. None of these before treasured things will exist. Smart workers will deploy all the global age wisdom of 'soft power asset management' issues in open boundary-less spaces, celestially wireless, global thinking with on-line high definition face to face execution. They will push buttons commands and controls, under the most optimum surrounding and magic will happen. This will leave behind mundane heavy office equipment and assembly line routines. The mundane work in cubical cages will be shifted to robotics and massive automation. The downtown office core of mega cities will match the weekend look every day. Most towers will transform into living spaces and theme driven jungles. Offices will start to disappear or turn into casual-crazy work spaces. They will be highly efficient, technologically advanced, economically informal, 24-7-365 access, designed like private clubs, rain forests, cafés or techie garages, to be used as and when required by anyone in the organization.

Beneficiaries: New global age smart workers with independence seeking adventures

Enemies: The last century mentality of job security and gold watch dependent retirements will be gone

Adjustments: Global age thinking to replace all routine and repeated work via automation will jump into being

Alternate Economy: The economical metamorphosis will start by new terminologies, new measurements and most importantly with the delivery of "True-Data" available all the time, real time and online. The alternate gig-economy will have billions of self-employed specialists around the clock on demand issues. The new types of UBER.HR will bring talent on demand, and Airbnb will provide required spaces; welcome to a new pure and raw talent based on round the clock 24x7x365 performance-economy.

Beneficiaries: The entrepreneurial side of global humanity currently squashed in chaos

Enemies: Ivory tower bastions and economic modeling based on pre-global age demands

Adjustments: Search truth via metadata and discover the power of simultaneous connectivity

Alternate Viewing: The world of Netflix has arrived. Mastery of streaming is new standard. Goodbye TV and repeated ads. The TV going dark is a symptom of a failed product that offered constant dumbed-down, often fake 'breaking news' blended with silly reality shows that are now being replaced by intelligent and customized rich content performances with instant online streaming access from all over the world. We can each create our own 'personalized on demand TV'. The primary sectors impacted will be the traditional TV journalism, advertising industry, mega streaming players, cable operators, global marketing and new personalized channels. The new world of streaming will create millions of micro-channels accessible via knowledge plugs.

Beneficiaries: Massive knowledge transfer via media tools

Enemies: Propogandist and advertising revenue centric mentality

Adjustments: Immediately submerge into new streaming culture and become an expert.

Alternate Commerce: The global age businesses, big or small, will develop special skills to deploy new deep and AI driven connectivity or face oblivion. The world is about to see an eruption of millions of new and powerful innovative ideas to amaze the global populace; daily gushes of amazing combinations, bustling with new collaborations and rapid deployment across the world, will emerge. Asia will be playing a very aggressive role. The entrepreneurial talent erupting form little towns and villages, entangled with technology with massive online interactions will become the norm; something that has never ever happened in the history.

Beneficiaries: New global age processing and advance level incubation of business ideas.

Enemies: Bureaucracy and old hierarchies, frozen minds and dull operators.

Adjustments: Without a Czar of AI you are working for an already dead organization.

When Innovation Becomes Suffocation? Innovation at best is like a water sprinkler on a nice healthy plant, making it grow and blossom; however, sprinkling without the plant is just like watering sand. Nothing happens.

Innovative excellence is the most critical component of creating grassroots prosperity in any country

Example: If flying a kite was a test of innovative excellence then making a kite requires an entrepreneur and an innovative team to make and deploy the thread. Such precise combinations, with the right skills, provide the actual kite flying experience. The lift and the somersault actions necessary to fly high and conquer the sky must exist in order to execute the novel plans. Without the kite, innovations teams are just holding the thread glaring at the future and pretending to fly a kite.

Fact: The last 100 earth shattering commercializations were delivered by entrepreneurs and almost all of them were often rejected by leading academic and financial experts. The entrepreneurial leadership is critically mandatory to any commercialization of any size, followed by a brilliant team to lead the pack with innovative excellence.

How to mobilize Professional Innovative talents across a nation?

Millions of high-quality entrepreneurs all over the world are restless and anxious to park in friendly and safe geographies. They want a place where they can operate under affable incentives of taxes and special residencies. They also want the respectability of being labeled as real job creators. Nations that are ready and capable of structuring such massive initiatives can offer unlimited access to unlimited professional innovation experts completely free, unlimited, easy and free access across the country in every sector is automated and digitally alive.

Heads of State: seeking economic survival?

Nationalize Innovation; to create massive participation amongst leading communities of scientific, engineering, medical and special technologies with global age skills; make all government initiatives freely available to all entrepreneurs across the nation. These programs must eliminate any complicated 20-page plus forms attached with twisted obligations. No matter how crazy and odd the concepts sound just support them with full confidence and officiate National Entrepreneurial Manifesto. Recognize all entrepreneurs of all sizes and types with varying success and history and declare them the most valuable asset of the nation. This free and unrestricted access will mobilize an entrepreneurial revolution and create massive grassroots prosperity but not the other way around where government sponsored innovative programs are bogged down in bureaucratic rules and regulations. Great academic and scientific talents linger behind expansive and cumbersome Ivy league halls.

Open and free maximum participation without entry fee will create collaborative win-win models. Imagine, 10,000 Entrepreneurs working on 10,000 projects with some 5000 Professional Innovation Experts deploying their knowledge along the way. This kind of thinking will change the dynamics of the local mid-size economy within a nation.

Study the world map daily and circumnavigate the earth slowly.

Making the World Prosperous Again

The dust bowls of recent economic developments are living proof of the mountains of bureaucracies and valleys of incompetence. Most of the dust storms were forecasted but were ignored.

The National Entrepreneurial Manifesto; or the so called essential "business plan of a nation",

Reality Check:

There is no single country in the world today that is powerful, smart or moral enough to take care of the rest of the world.

Fact: The world is teetering and ready to slide into a new global financial crisis.

Fact: Leading governments, at best, are silent and avoiding real hot topics.

Fact: Never before has the socio-economic melting points been so high, while growth is so low.

No other experiment of human endeavor has been as successful as America.

Smart Nations:

Where common sense dominates rhetoric, where smart work is rewarded, global execution accepted and transformational of all aspects are considered absolute priority.

Smart nations will not be 'classroom-trained' but rather 'occupationally-trained'.

To balance an 'Entrepreneurial Manifesto for Nation' a solid understanding of occupationally-trained, with global age skills is an absolute prerequisite.

Entrepreneurialism is not a course, a degree or a written methodology; it's all about understanding and experiences acquired by real living encounters; it's not 'explicit knowledge' like learning accounting, but rather 'tacit knowledge' like learning to swim or ride a bike.

Human development is not measured in just degrees and certifications but rather in gaining real occupational expertise and transformational entrepreneurialism. Education is at its best when left alone to simply grow. Real life occupational experiences are best in the economical battlefields where creating prosperity and job creation are the prime goals of creating grassroots prosperity.

We already have an overly educated and certified population with extremely under-experienced youth population amongst all of the developed nations. What's next?

No new budgets required:

Most of the above do not require new special budgets or massive funding but rather a deeper understanding of key issues of deployment, mobilization and global age execution. Most of the infrastructure is already there and all it requires is rapid mobilization.

Fact: The world can easily absorb unlimited exportable ideas in unlimited vertical markets.

Fact: The well-designed innovative ideas are worthy of such quadrupled volumes.

Fact: The entrepreneurial and dormant talents of a nation are capable of such tasks.

Fact: The new global age skills, knowledge and execution are now the most critical and missing links.

Question: As a national agenda, is the leadership ready to engage and debate with world-class thought leadership on such crucial prosperity and job-creation topics at the highest level and then share the results openly with the nation? Is the Local or National leadership ready to recognize such optimized and hidden entrepreneurial talents as the biggest and most timely assets of the nation?

New separation and new divides:

The new prosperity demands a brand-new space to house such new thinking and new styles of business structures.

A complete separation from the old systems and thinking must take place. The start of the E-commerce revolution flourished with a brand-new set of rules, new procedures, completely new looks and new types of staff on brand new floors, with special thinking and skills. The E-commerce revolution was never an extension of the previous industrial revolution. It was a brand-new umbrella, far superior in thinking and execution. Without brand new separate facilities, new styles of teams and new protocols, e-commerce would have collapsed on greasy factory floors and would have been misfiled in old secretarial pools. The old management like viruses were separated, old contagious mentalities were blocked and restricted, and only newly trained and qualified IT specialist had around the clock access to the air-conditioned humming rooms working as the new pulsating hearts of the innovative organizations. This was prevalent across the corporate world and began its function very recently during the isolated main frame computer era.

Unless frequent flyers are pulled out of the cockpits and replaced by real professional pilots we cannot land safely. The grassroots prosperity failures of past era can no longer be solved by the same system and leadership that created them. A brand-new page and new teams in new locations are mandatory.

Today's deniers are now the new enemy of growth; fake media is now the new enemy of the nation, and the incompetency the new burden to new transformation. We must quickly identify, isolate, transform and move forward.

The New Challenges of Beyond 2020

Collaborative synthesizim has arrived in full swing. Feel the rhythm; learn the new dance, enjoy the beat and musicology of new free technologies and the let the spectators watch.

Arrange a bold and open debate, create a small but high-profile forum, and debate, engage and fight out in the open; spin hard so it finally curds into something solid. It's not important who is right or wrong; what is important is the real truth. We must continually seek to find why the truth is so hidden, and why solutions are so prohibited. It will not be an easy process. Courage and stamina will be mandatory.

Discover and define economic nationalism. Make your own country great by first adopting a positive and logical approach to national prosperity. Discover how to work successfully with one country and later multiply such skills to expand to hundreds of new countries. Fair trading is wide open all over the world. Boycotts and closed trade are destructive thinking, caused by globalization based on serving only selected groups. Mankind wants to depend on its natural survival strategy and has now figured out that enough is enough and the time for big change has already arrived.

Global debates and discussions on prosperity roads

The new global age world is slowly starting to talk, soon it will walk and if things work as they should it will run.

Suddenly, the masses of the world seem to have acquired their own internet-doctorates on intricate histories and diverse geographies with the latest social media gossip. These bursts of new global awareness are intertwined with the new and unwinding future. It's good; the awareness is making their life choices easier; they are getting informed and can make their own decisions. While surrounded by dogmatic implications and economical fog, their certification primarily delivered by the free internet browsing curriculum, they are now talking. They are knowledge rich and skilled enough to read between the lines. They can differentiate between destructive deployments of human talent directed towards hurting mankind and ignoring constructive models of real extreme value creation as sustainable economic models of prosperity. The big change is on the horizon and it appears unstoppable.

Today, global affairs and international issues are routinely being debated; sound bites are considered fake news, while the absence of wisdom and integrity in debates are proof of being trapped in swamps. Whether it's pointing North, South, East or West, no matter where; the post-Trump, post-Media and post-West universe is now becoming common and they are filled with open topics. The world is finally learning to talk boldly and openly.

If the super success of India and China were considered a surprise, the rest of the world must be both deaf and blind. The wild goose chases and openly visible economical fiascos of Western economies were simply more or less fireworks of lights and thundering sounds. It was all visible on the common streets.

The fireworks were the illusion; the strategy was political deceptions, democratically deployed in the open, making destructive thinking visible while creating crumbling economies and infrastructures. Massive dissatisfaction at the grassroots levels are all real proof of dysfunctional operations. The most damaging sign was the lack of focused and bold dialogues, debates and intellectual forums. These are needed in order to crack open the truth and real issues; teleprompter dependent lip service and photo-op events fill the media and are frequently only deep and silent chasms that fill each day. Historically, and especially during the last couple of millennia, such prolonged negligence brought dynasties to ruins.

Today's global age world has become very capable of recognizing brutal dictatorships, repressed nations or brainwashed nations; the political correctness media worshipping nations, where truth is taboo, the scared nations where they see the world as the enemy or where teleprompter dependent leaderships selling fake prosperity will fail in coming elections.

As a consequence, a very wide-awake world is making fine-tuned adjustments and the global populace is in unison. This has never happened before in the history and the world is so ready to make some positive changes.

Survival of the fittest will now be measured by what a person can do to survive in the tides of fakery. Honest work and value creation will save mankind. Once truth is known, the lies will stand out. only mental and physical stamina to cope with such factors will now determine survivability. Lower-end societies cannot be fixed by the destruction of upper-end societies, but by fair and balanced distributions.

Keeping awake at night?

The current deafening noise and out of sync confusion amongst people raging in some 100,000 cities and towns of the world is living proof of disconnected and divisive life styles. The silent voice of the global alpha dreamers, the silent murmur of emerging economies and the silent restlessness of global citizenry, are all poised to create better and more harmonious times, and isolate fakery.

Beyond 2020 a typical single $1000-dollar investment in technology will eliminate a single $100,000 yearly executive job forever.

By 2020 and beyond, some three billion workers will be exposed to a new "workless-world" impacting local grassroots prosperity.

By 2020 a new world will emerge; a digitally flat world; but clearly divided between smartly informed nations and propagandized nations; economically flat world; but critically divided on inequalities and serving special interests

It's not that the economy is falling, it's the political intelligence that's not rising.

It's not the future that appears too dark; it's the brightness of imagination that's too dim

It's not the people that can't get peace, it's the agenda centricity that can't get enough wars

The time for small change has past.

Time for massive transformational revolutions is simmering.

The time to mobilize entrepreneurialism has arrived.

Chapter Seventeen

Imagination has no form but vision has its own weight, balance and structure and global vision for creating iconic ideas is the ultimate

Strategy Ten: Image supremacy protocols

Definition: Mastery of global image positioning.

Usage: How to lead across national and global marketplace creating intellectual property assets.

Symptoms: Lack of understanding of superiority of image and identity in the global marketplace and extreme value creation and image generation protocols, being stuck in decades old logo-slogan mentality

The above ten top critical components to provide wings to any great iconic ideas are explained in great details in the following chapters.

Mastery of global stage

Should we only target our local customer base and ignore the world? Idea positioning on global stage and understanding mastery of image supremacy protocols. How critical is it for you to drive your campaigns on national or global stage with mastery of Image Supremacy Protocols? Something under a program of learning may take few weeks to a few months. This advance level will give you power of extreme value creation and equally extreme image generation as when both deployed to enter the upper stratosphere of productivity, performance and profitability

There are rules and laws to ensure national and global image supremacy of innovative excellence. Deeper study can provide some depth and eventually mastery. It will open powerful options and new windows for global expansion. Explore how this can help you and take you to the upper stratosphere. It's your call; it is conquering the supremacy of innovation or lose out completely.

Understanding of global image will make you the architect of phenomenon marvels. This is all about extreme value creation, paralleled with extreme image generation so that the building at completion will stand tall and visible under the spotlight. Your ideas become part of the successful legend while making great productivity, high-quality performance and profitability

When all of the above ten key components are used as raw material, your new ideas will flourish and amazing thing happen. The bottom-line is that it is a matter of personal choice; there are always two options, just survive or build.

Now, that you have fully grasped the architectural needs required for building of your idea, let's study each building components in details and face the current realities on each and study each component's hidden and obvious features, followed by some suggestions that may become your surprise for everyone.

Learn to unlearn. This is all about mental readjustment, like taking inventory inside a large warehouse or arranging furniture in a massive drawing room. Our over busy lives entangled in chaos do not allow us a lot of time to rethink things. Practice and guidance gives us mastery. We must continually question how we operate; we must take time to think about what and how we want to build. How quickly can one learn to unlearn; here are some ideas for speedy process

Make a list of the top ten extraordinary skills you have; list them in priority and then determine which one of them you would eliminate in order to get new replacements. There is no need to worry because nothing will be erased or disappear from your imagination. Nothing will be removed, because your knowledge as an engineer, scientist, activist, event organizer, or concert pianist will NEVER disappear.

This is all about thinking and exploring your inner self. It's just to prepare your mind to acknowledge, accept and relearn that it can create new ideas. Your brain has lots of space for previous knowledge and skill and for whatever new ideas you may wish to add. Once you take inventory, you may discover that the things you considered important all along may now not be THAT important any longer.

The mind is limitless in every way. It can design a hockey stick or it can develop a mission to Mars. The mind expands if we direct it to do so; it just needs new directions in order to move into subconscious terrain. Like any mental exercises, from High School to PhD, it keeps expanding; it can stretch; it's endlessly expandable. It has the photographic memory of the millions of moves for a chess player all beautifully laid out in a winnable sequence, or the billions of notes in precise sequence needed for the conductor in order to produce timelines and synchronized sound. It is easy to fall into patterns of thinking, patterns that do not question or help us expand our thinking. Now it is time to restart, retrain and   unlearn your mind and use all the space in order to start selecting new thinking and ideas. The new relearning process will not be easy, but it will pay off in leaps and bounds. The most difficult process is always the first step. The rest becomes easy and second nature.

Chase the truth, because you are hard wired for the long pursuit, just seek out the lies around you, then analyze and eliminate them. Acquire new energy and confidence. Living with lies will often take you to territories that will not deliver the truths needed for real building of new ideas.

Become reason centric and pursue passion and march proudly to your goals. Realize that this provides you the most of happiness and ignore the common rat race roads of just material wealth, which is often a shallow vision.

You will need a blueprint, a complete landscape, where you must identify your position so as to justify your standing and reasons to be there. You must have the passion to march in one of the million options of directions. Make your mind your friend and help it to guide you. Make your heart the beacon of light that will assure you to stay on the right track.

One lesson, one step, one action, will take you nowhere. Ask aloud, what are you really doing? Ask why and when, periodically or occasionally, casually or formally, alone or under guidance, sometimes, or all the times-- this is how you discover the hidden genius.

Only with questions will your hidden genius get awakened and start opening your undiscovered talents and show new paths. A brand-new level of superior confidence will start to appear and positive attitude start becoming the norm.

Boredom and tiredness are common basic earthly problems, and this is when the body does all the chores and the mind shuts-off and becomes a secondary element of the physiology. But when you are constantly using your mind and let the mind manage your life, you enter into limitless energy and a state of relaxation and are able to only focus on your goals. When you enter this state of being, you can monitor your depth and advancements.

Nothing will happen, unless you reason and master organized thinking

Start thinking by discovering what thinking is all about in the first place; it may take weeks or months, or years but you are never too late, never too young or old. Increase your depth with organized and productive thinking, and once you reach the point where you are continually and deliberately pondering your every movement, you will know that you have arrived. The beauty is that you will not get frustrated at every little thing. Nothing will bother you because it will be just another challenge for you to tackle with superior imagination. Small talk of small realm will have little concern to you; you will now strive for superior-level complexity and face storms without fear, like a warrior. At this stage you will know your powers. Furthermore, you will not get headaches because of too much thinking. You will get a sense of freedom in its place. When you reach the point where you are always thinking in constructive formats, always reflecting, always weighing the pros and cons, you will be liberated and your body will be refreshed with vigor, strength and high energy levels. Your "can do" attitude will lead to happiness and contentment.

Now let's enlarge the scope, let's bring the enterprise components.

The image supremacy of innovative excellence

Image Supremacy, the art of getting under global spotlights. No big or small empire of any kind located anywhere in the world will acquire the prestigious shine and luster without fully understanding the hidden powers of image supremacy protocols. This is an advanced game for the already successful wishing to enter the upper stratosphere.

Successful programs like TQM, Balance Scorecard and Six Sigma dramatically improve quality and performance. They are designed to rightfully calibrate the hard asset issues of production. There is a serious lack of three-dimensional modeling for soft issues, like innovative thinking and the dimensions of the core vision itself enveloping all production issues. These image supremacy rules challenge current methods and offer checklists to assess the need of newer, softer and special agenda-centric approaches.

Corporations engaged in innovation and seeking image supremacy must embrace both sides of the equation: the hard asset issues, like productions, material and costs along with soft asset issues, like vision, creative ideas combined with hidden talents blended with desires and emotions.

Bending pipes to make a perfect chair is a very noble innovation, but equally important are the mind-bending exercises in the boardrooms that are necessary to create an innovative culture throughout the organization. Most organizations use innovation like a last-minute bandage. Lack of sales and competition from others with innovation flag and newer models cannot be healed with band aids.

Quick fix innovations lead to quicksand. Ideally, they would be better off doing nothing; take a deep pause, retreat internally, start an evaluation leading to a revolution and strive to become a totally innovative organization driven by the creative depths of their own core vision. This way, they have a better chance to become shockingly powerful.

Here are the quick measurements as scorecards to determine your own needs for better calibration towards progress.

The Scorecard

When was the last time you organized a board meeting just to discuss the soft-assets of the organization?

What are the top five questions every management member knows but dares not ask?

Why is the organization making only 'pants' but not 'jackets' or vice-versa?

Why does the organization have too many or too few brands?

Why is the organization headed in a particular direction and what will it take to change course?

The innovation nomenclature

Increasingly often corporate nomenclature is used to create the sensation of innovation, 'Nova this' and 'New that'. The 'inno' based names primarily created to attract end user attention are already highly diluted. The excessive usage of the term 'innovation' often grafted in anticipation of sudden blossom reveals voids and chasms in the core vision, where the fogged illusion of invention clashes with market realities. If you could ever see a crystallized version of a truly innovative corporate vision, its middle core would be embalmed with molten lava to continuously energize innovation. Gravity defying organizations like Apple, Google, BMW, Facebook, Virgin or Tata, for example, make up a minuscule percentage of the successful global businesses and clearly point to the remaining majority for running on somewhat entirely different types of treadmills.

Innovation is the single most important missing component among organized business all over the world. An easy parallel can be drawn to "I.T.", a term that has also lost some of its power and meaning and became a loose expression that fits any situation. What is IT today? It involves the use of the iPad, Cloud computing, Excel, Internet, or driving with GPS? It's all around us but not 'everybody' is in IT. Depending on the nature, type, style and size of the operation business, nomenclature must address and clarify by whom and where 'true innovation' is being applied. Despite all the PR claims, not every claimant is into true innovation.

The scorecard

In how many different places does the organization promote the word 'innovation' and how many times correctly?

How often does the entire organization go through an 'innovation audit'?

How rapidly is the market share increasing due to the new innovation talks?

What percentage of the staff is really committed to new innovation and why?

The innovative culture

True innovative culture can be created when both the hard asset issues and soft asset issues blend within the organization – such overlays create dramatic results. When a corporate mandate boldly acknowledges both soft and hard issues as two parallel dynamics throughout every aspect of production, and encourages companywide dual-application, will the result can be an groundswell at the grassroots level. This proves to be far more productive over traditional practices like framing mission statements and hanging them in each cubicle.

To capture the hidden magic, knowledge from the best innovation consultants, experts, designers and provocateurs can tackle this apparently impossible task. This is where the acid test comes into play; vision is a soft asset issue and so is innovative thinking. Both soft issues must become visible for the top teams. Only upon comfortably conquering both sides of the equation, where hard and soft assets issues are simultaneously overlaid, can optimum performance commence. Hence, the supremacy of innovation becomes demonstrable and such movements can change the rigidness in attitudes, especially in a totally hard-asset-based-mentality.

Vision, on the other hand is far too complicated and difficult to map out when modeling its dimensions and applicability. Vision sometimes acts as an immense magnet, attracting all kinds of fly-by ideas – whether metallic splinters or full-sized objects, these ideas cling and, over time, distort the original shape of the magnet.

Welcome to the world of artificial-innovation-incubation where ideas are adopted without logical or creative soft issue base while rigid production creates illusionary progress. Most organizations approach innovation by mixing good and bad ideas with good and bad processes and hope for the best. Basically, without the "do or die" passion of the innovative thinking the road appears confusing and bumpy. The power of vision must be harnessed and therefore soft asset modeling is one way to measure its power.

The scorecard

How often do the hardcore engineers and best creative minds share ideas?

How often do the top leaders talk about core vision and invite challengers?

How often do the innovative ideas, discussion and changes appear effortless and part of culture?

How often does the leadership attempt to chart vision as a three-dimensional model like any other production challenge?

Surviving in the current age of abundance as opposed to the past age of scarcity when simple tinkering with the product was considered innovative, requires360-degree, and upside-down turns. Constructing a dynamic, innovation-friendly and manageable environment means the corporate culture must use both its hard and soft assets and create a new, balanced mentality. This double-barreled audit approach allows for successful staging of the following key procedures to ensure dynamic debates, pragmatic solutions and definite improvement towards added 'value creation' and 'image expansion'

Crystallization of the vision: If vision is the ultimate source of all inspiration, then this vision, as a soft issue, must be openly accepted as a soft-asset-issue that together with added layers of hard-asset issues creates a three-dimensional model. Such calibrations of hard and soft issues allow all teams to touch and feel the direction and goals of the enterprise.

Ignition of hidden talent: If human talent is the place where all the good ideas are processed and fertilized, then talented feedback must be boldly accepted and moreover, encouraged in all phases of production, whether we are speaking of tangible goods or services. If implemented correctly, such changes will ensure both competitive advantages and better team performance.

Extreme value creation: If your current offerings are already considered "best in class", then taking an intellectual hammer and literally smashing them into finite pieces and later hanging them in the middle of the boardroom will germinate the ideas for extreme value creation. Drastic innovation demands drastic measures. The future belongs to the bold.

Extreme image generation: If your current innovations are not getting traction, flip the coin. Image and name identity constitute the glue that binds the elements of success. Even the greatest innovations can, at times, get lost in twisted name identities, confusing customers and therefore dissipating in global cyber media, or get drowned via wrongly positioned commercials, logos and graphics killing the essence of the product, service or business.

Garden of money trees: If your successful and highly innovative products and services are not creating a garden of money trees, chop them down. The beauty and pleasure of working in a truly high value generation enterprise is to witness the ripening of the fine fruits of success. Seek out all the wisdom and knowledge, get the best innovation experts and train your entire organization to think of innovation as its core competence. Innovation is not about a sudden change but about change in continuous motion.

Image supremacy of innovation: If your teams are naturally inclined to place soft assets issues before hard asset issues and can boldly face the outcomes, certain supremacy will surface. The finite spectrum will be harnessed, the quality and logic will combine and image will come under global spotlight. This is easier said than done, and the bearer of the vision must be in full participatory mode right from the start, otherwise the fog creeps in and illusions start showing.

These six stages may vary depending on the style and size of the organization but they conclusively lay out winning combination and will make the hidden entrapments come to surface. It's important to note that all such soft procedures have to deal with the following friendly or hostile realties.

The adjustments, create a list of the top 100 soft issue-related questions that you think your organization will be most reluctant to answer. Link the answers back to hard asset capabilities. Then, create a companywide debate and seek consensus; look at the issues from all angles – inside and out.

Next, if you are not already the 'innovation thinking' tsar for the organization, circulate a memo today and have the best one appointed before the end of the month.

Anything less will keep you stuck in mediocrity.

The supremacy of innovation is highly logical and achievable process. Thought it tends to slant towards soft asset issues, it cannot be successful without full hard asset support.

Power of words

Words are the voices of our thoughts, without words we have no thoughts. Example, close your eyes, imagine A few words. Now take a moment to recognize in your mind the meaning and physicality of these words. Now erase these words completely as if you never knew them and now try to imagine and convey this same thought. Try to see without words; if there are no words in subconsciousness there will be no thought and no communication. The more words we know the better becomes our thinking. Deeper understandings and better definitions of words are what drives our communications. The more precise is your understanding of the word the sharper is its definition and usage. The better the sequencing of the words the clearer the message. The better the alignment of meaning of words the more attractive is the message. This is how communication is advanced. This how new thought leadership is formed.

So how do you create deeper thought? It is not by just assembling a lot of impressive words but by having a logical recall of well understood words from your reservoir of experiences. Depth of knowledge gives power to the words. Now you have to realize all words known to you are hidden in the bottom of your consciousness and ask why only special ones come to you as 'recall' at the right time of thinking and decision making. Make a point to study this subject deeply. Explore your language skills and take interest in linguistics to improve your thinking. Memorability of a word is the most powerful tool in the world of corporate communication and marketing No other place is as strategically powerful where carefully crafted naming for a business, or products and services and well-structured names are used so that not only such name-brands become powerful assets but also because they are capable of immediate recall. Imagine a product or a service in any area and the name that pops up is the reason of their success. Billions of other names just die out screaming for attention. It's an art and a science to understand corporate nomenclature and how business names are created. This is not to be confused with logo-slogan driven agencies; this being nomenclature of business names is a very advanced level space of linguistics and global usage of words, alphabets and structures and their connotations. To become a better thinker become more familiar with linguistics.

Right questions will lead to right answers and right answers will lead to wisdom. Wisdom is not just knowledge; it's more about how to use knowledge; education only burdens you with knowledge, but self-discovery enlightens you with more wisdom. Knowledge shows what's right and what's wrong, but wisdom allows you to select between the right and the wrong.

The fourteen dimensions of image supremacy protocols

Excerpted from Image Supremacy, Metrostate, by Naseem Javed, 2013

Pyramid of Power: The Syllabus of the full year program on Image Supremacy Protocols, is packed and holds the secrets to Image Supremacy, deployment and execution plans. It is important to structurally visualize the parts and understand their inter play. This set of tools can easily be applied to any business, Nation, or organization. The building blocks for Image Supremacy are:

The Pyramids of Power: The four key hierarchies that provide equilibrium and a path to power

The Spheres of Success: Measures interactive and perpetual motions of the organization. Evaluates the survivability of planned directions. Contains four key elements wedged against each other; these elements spin against external forces and provide avenues for increased success.

The Cubes of Stardom: Creates a dynamic interactive e___nvironment that can be seen and touched by everyone involved. There are six interdependent and parallel dimensions to stardom.

The 100 Tasks: The steps that are needed in order to reach Image Supremacy within each of the Fourteen Protocols.

The Fourteen Protocols:

The Blue prints to better prosperity via creating enterprises

The Pyramids of Power: See the image of a powerful pyramid; it is hierarchal with an extremely strong base that towers upward, reaching for the sky. The four parts of the Pyramids of Power will help us see how, from the super strong base with layers, we will identify current status. It will also help us find future challenges as we work our way toward the top and to Image Supremacy. The support sides of the pyramid are the first four protocols:

The Ownership Hierarchy—Originality
The Operational Hierarchy—Focus
The Value Hierarchy—Passion
The Image Hierarchy—Longevity
Spheres of Success

Once the Pyramids of Power have been determined and the ground work for Image Supremacy has been laid, we are ready to begin the Spheres of Success. Envision the shape of a sphere; it is like a ball, a globe or the planet Earth. It rolls along looking for possible obstructions and opportunities. This component will help us evaluate and determine the survivability of our Image Supremacy plan's directions.

The following four elements will spin against external forces, and look inward and outward as it moves in order to increases our chances for success:

The Sphere of Innovation—Adaptability
The Sphere of Marketing—Presence
The Sphere of Promise—Integrity
The Sphere of Finance—Opportunity

Cubes of Stardom

We will use the Cubes of Stardom to identify and plot six aspects of the plan and to create a dynamic interactive environment where all participants become totally involved. Again, clearly see the image; it is a cube with both horizontal, vertical, and depth dimensions. It has six congruent faces which give it strength. Its faces are interdependent and complement each other. Its six faces and the dimensions to stardom are:

Dimension of Nomenclature—Individuality
Dimensions of Global Expansion—Vision
Dimensions of 24/7/365—Dynamics
Dimensions of Digitization—Compression
Dimensions of Customers—Selling
Dimensions of Teams—Trust

Summary

It is important that all of us fully understand all fourteen Protocols—what they are and how they interact. However, it is essential that we can thoroughly function and be an "expert" within one of the Team structures of the Protocols identified below:
How critical is it for you to drive your campaigns on national or global stage with mastery of image supremacy Protocols? Something under a program of learning may take few weeks to a few months. This advance level will give you power of extreme value creation and equally extreme image generation as when both deployed to enter the upper stratosphere of productivity, performance and profitability. Full program
www.imagesupremacy.com

Conversations with your mind

To train your mind to stop thinking is almost an impossible task; however, practicing to stop thinking may provide some new additional strength towards achieving clarity, resulting in better decision making and freshness of thoughts. The mind is always alive and always working; but without focus having an overly busy mind is more like having a very large garbage dump. What you really need is something like a jug of clean water that is always ready to pour. The brain must be ready for focused thinking. It may take months, years or decades, to train the brain for this kind of response, but this is a great way to stretch mental stamina, get new mental calmness so you can redirect for new energies.

Just stop thinking for few minutes several times a day and this will be a start. If you see something that you do not like start seeing it with your mind. If you hear something that you do not like start exploring its sound and meaning If you feel anxious or stressed ask your mind to help you reach calmness. With practice and repeated use, the brain can't achieve anything, All your physiology is controlled by your own mind. Superior performance of the body is hidden in your mind, not in the body. Study Olympic Gold Medalists So, explore your own dietary mind and not dietary foods. Your own discovery is your number one challenge. Your own extreme value creation is already hidden inside you. Why?

Just work hard and class-room education may simply put you behind. Today, hard work has less value, over smart work. Today, Universities have less value over Internet-street-smartness, entrepreneurial smartness, global age smartness. To become part of the Top 1% wealth club is just not easy, either you are born into and get pulled into it. It depends either on your premium university access or via spousal arrangement. The rest is just grinding on the other side of the tracks.

The other option is to build something of amazing value that will cata‑ pult you into that 1% percentile club. So, either you build or just survive; either way, it's always your option, your choice and your performance.

Complaining about other people's wealth and about equality is pure nonsense. It will be best to just wake up and prove yourself.

ARE you an alpha dreamer? Let's explore further...

Critical Criteria on Global Image

Creating soft power assets and Intellectual Property like having globally workable and protectable identities as most valuable assets of an organization is an art and a science. Not to be confused with massive advertising and promotion of name brands. Name identities which are already shared as similar names with thousands of others are not the winners. Individualistic icons like Sony, Google, Facebook, Telus are in a very special space where boardroom maneuvers and legal-linguistic strategies come into play.

If a product is worthy of one of a kind identity and protection so be it. If a corporation is worthy of ownership of that name identity with 100% exclusivity by its owners and not shared by hundreds and thousands of other sound-alike or look-alike names, a very advanced level process comes into play.

The powerbrokers of the world organizations seeking powerful image positioning are clearly divided in two group those who know and play by the rules and keep winning and others who have no idea on even how and where such rules exist and keep losing. But why?

Advanced studies are critical

Chapter Eighteen

Mistakes add amazing patterns on the tapestry of success

Superiority on profitability

The Change factor; In so many styles and so many different messages, most of the above lines have been written by thousands of geniuses during the last hundred years, but still it is as if for some mysterious reason the simple black and white rules simply do not stick.

The successful models of individual performances and of very successful enterprises are clearly available in broad day light, but it's all about OUR own limits that prohibit our own self-discovery and keep our own hidden talents from bringing us to victory. It's the lingering of our own incompetency longing for the comfort zones of yesterday that lead to new fears of tomorrow's landscapes.

Put in the self-discovery hours, do the serious uplifting work, optimize talents or just be quiet. No more complaints.

New heights via self-discovery

Critical exercise: This is how you will reach new heights, all by yourself, via self-discovery. Imagine you are in room, all alone, standing in the center, where all the entire walls are mirrors and there are dozens of reflections of you all around you in that room. Now imagine that you can remove each of those reflections one by one until there is only one left. This is you.

Right now, this very second, as you read, there are hundreds of such reflections, all around you, from family and friends to corporate to social media plus your own projected persona. Also realize that you leave hundreds of reflections as you go out and live a normal day. Like, what you think who you are, what others think you are, and what you actually are. You must be cognizant of such perceptions and factors.

Now dig deep and try to identify these reflections, their causes and meanings; they all lead to some clarity and slowly with better understanding of who you really are. Some surprises will appear as you become aware of such notions. The biggest confidence gainer is self-discovery. If you only knew what has been hidden inside you. Early schooling, based on the last century mentality, teaches us how to discover the world outside of us and nothing is given to help us discover about what is inside us. Self-discovery is essential in order to move forward. History and geography are important enough but not when it's critically essential to discovering ourselves first. Self-discovery was almost taboo for fears of creating smarter populations. The Dogmas were threatened. Hence self-discovery was isolated for Prophets in their favorite caves and super arched over-grown trees. The first period of every school across the world, every single day should begin with a calm set-up with a silent focus on the discovery of who we are and what's already inside us. In most cases children are far smarter than teachers, and that is another reason for not asking tiny Billy to explain his thinking. Just stick to 'Baba baba black sheep' and be quiet.

This self-discovery is not easy, but in can be the most joyous journey for any age. Try it for few months or few years and all will become second nature with amazing results. Remember these are all free and effortless mental stretching.

Critical Exercise: Sit in a quiet room with complete silence and in complete isolation thinking of anything but paying attention to the voice coming from your head. Now imaging that this voice was not in your head but coming from the outside. This may take months to years. Now try to establish the origin and the source of that voice and start paying more attention to its wisdom. This is you as its your voice and your wisdom. Some of this is known and some unknown. All this will take months, eventually you reach a stage where you engage in with a question and discover that what you questioned and what was answered was totally unexpected. You are now discovering your deep inner voices and clarity of thinking. You are now in a very advanced stage of learning the unexpected and high-quality self-optimization, leading to higher productivity and creating superior performance.

Critical Exercise: sit on a bench in a park, and look out as you keep your eyes open but ask your mind and eyes to see nothing, just look even if it was the park or a white wall while telling your mind and eyes to stay open but seeing nothing. Not a stare, not a glance, just a look. It's difficult, but something will happen, look as you were looking but still not seeing anything. In a few minutes you will discover that you are seeing something that you never saw before, because when you look at the ducks at the pond you mind is focused on the ducks in the pond; when we are seeing all of the pond and telling the active mind to ignore anything and everything in front of you and making it almost invisible. You are asking your mind to un-focus. Now your mind and eyes can see things that your conscious mind never saw before because it was obeying your intuitions, reasons or causes. Relax, you have already done this thousands of times when sitting idle and drifting in thoughts; you were looking sideways without paying attention, when suddenly a bird lands in your periphery vision. You jump and notice. This is all about training your eyes to see beyond the normal and find exceptional details. This is all about self-discovery.

These exercises to optimize the building of new ideas, here, you will acquire some level of mastery and some more knowledge, but the big lesson here is you do not require mastery of each but deeper understanding. Like an architect you are very good at few aspects and have good knowledge on others to call upon the best players to cover for the rest. The worst situation is having mastery of none and just being jack ass of all will simply not cut it. Self-discovery and self-optimization will teach you all that and help with new powers of thinking.

Creating Prosperity Roads: Taking your ideas on world stage. Now you are ready to go very big and you will see how your mind envision this.

Creating an enterprise leads to prosperity. The roads to prosperity are straightforward, but they can be extremely rough. Whatever road your enterprise takes, the journey will be all about your self-discovery, self-optimization and endurance of your mental and emotional stamina.

Future enterprises will be primarily driven by mental powers and supported by almost free technologies. This was not the case last decade.

Understanding productivity, performance and profitability. The business world is filled with noises, chaos and screams; the noises for lack of productivity, chaos for lack and the screams for lack of profitability. Without productivity, performance and profitability a business has no purpose, value or any meaning. Although, these pursuits are very well understood all over the world, realty shows they are still considered almost impossible hurdles to overcome.

Perform like a symphonic orchestra

Why can't an organization perform like a symphonic orchestra and create music of profitability?

How can these concepts get fixed and what are the simple and pragmatic solutions for creating prosperity?

For example, in contrast to noises, chaos and screaming pursuant to enterprises, just listen to a nice Symphony.

Stop and take a break, a deep moment to listen or watch and understand how the actual music is being created. Right from the start, the symphony is captured in somebody's mind. Structured in a deliverable format, translated into musical notes, sequenced on paper, so it's translatable to hundreds of other musicians of the orchestra where each is given a particular indication of what to do at a particular time during the music execution process. No other model comes as close to running a large growing enterprise as does conducting a symphony. A business enterprise is nothing but a vision of its founder, clarified and translated into business plans shared with management teams where everybody is given special tasks and certain actions in order to reach synchronization with the master plan and create productivity, performance and profitability.

Deeply study the symphony and how an orchestra performs, most importantly in synchronization from start to finish. We must learn how to manage productivity, performance and profitability just like the orchestra produces the perfect symphony. It's that easy, but extremely difficult to achieve harmony, but why?

The most important aspect of a symphony is that the music is created as a 'State of Being'; it is almost effortless; it does not involve 200 musicians arguing and trying their own notes. It is rather produced as a state of being where all the notes and all the actions get combined to create the desired sound. While, in Fact each and every single strike of a note, a drum beat, or a bow on a string will make no sense at all if performed in isolation. This is basically what a large organization needs in real time because it's all about creating beauty in their performance from design, manufacturing, distribution, positioning and communications and packaging and all is completed in synchronic fashion. Anything crafted or perfected on its own will have no value. Observe orchestras and symphonies and understand why they appear so very effortless. Now, study the top successful business operations around the globe and how they operate on a similar process by having well organized teams, well-trained people, meticulously planned procedures and processes with controls to make sure that everything gets connected at the right time, at the right place and for the right reasons. With vision, plans, precision, accuracy, and controls all aspects are covered and for these reasons all such enterprises generate productivity, performance, with profitability as their reward.

If this was just a matter of listening to some symphonies and studying how they work and then creating similar procedures for commercial organization to make it happen, what is the secret, where is the problem; where is the mystery and why there is so much noise, chaos, and screaming?

Because, it is extremely, extremely difficult

An orchestra consists of highly specialized instruments developed over centuries, and each instrument has its own set of rules to operate and practice. The players love their instruments and have emotional attachments in achieving mastery of performance. Each is player willing to play precise notes as prescribed by the music score. All of the players know that otherwise wrong notes will only create noise. The most critical part is that each person is fully aware of the entire symphony and not only their own notes, they know what others are doing to achieve final delivery of music. This assembly of few hundred musicians in simultaneous synchronization, under a master conductor creates an amazing sound, because there is a pre-understood game plan being executed meticulously.

Running of organizations is no different

Two questions; firstly, is the organization interested in creating a large maneuver that could operate smoothly and function like a synchronized orchestra in order to produce profitability? Secondly, is the leadership willing to take its vision, like the music score, share it with all team members, and distribute all of the sheets of music to all the musicians so that each team member knows their special role in the process? The team members can then practice, clarify and organize a combined level of superior performance capability and continue the refinement process in order to achieve superior delivery of performance on a continuous basis.

At this point, it is essential to study corporate symphonia and how such similarities are intertwined. It is very logical and a simple way to advance. It can be done, why not, but it's not that easy, let's explore at the micro-level

Just like instruments, every layer of corporate departments has developed guidelines and execution plans over centuries. Finance, production, manufacturing, marketing, or corporate management rules have been developed and demand perfected execution with full knowledge of the game plan. The problem is that these fine instruments of execution and deployments need mastery from the management players. Each player must fully grasp the big picture on where the corporate enterprise is headed and fully understand their role in the entire process. They must know how and why and when it will generate the music of profitability. Less than 1% of the businesses around the world have such control, mastery, and complete transparency in operation. The rest are mostly tangled, hitting great notes at the wrong times or bad notes at right times, creating noise, chaos and eventually screams for profitability.

Local games

Critical steps to create local economic miracles and corporations can play expanded roles. Every big and small enterprise, right across the nation should be allowed free access to massive national digital platforms to unable cross-fertilization and showcase their talents, goods and services. This national and global exposure with world-class quality will create trading opportunities and will mobilize the dormant regions. Every big and small, young and old, men and women entrepreneurs of the nation to be allowed to showcase their talent ideas, no matter how big or small but recognized to be part of custom designed national platform.

Every national trade association and every major chamber of commerce across the nation to be mandated to share such national umbrella platforms with cross-fertilization and large pools of knowledge shared to enable vertical sector growths. All this activity will further enhance already structured trade groups via fast digital to open flood gates to new global customers. Not to be confused with current newsletter and broken mailing lists, this is very advanced footwork on global stage. Digitalization will open a brand-new world for those missing global accessibility and limited on showcasing of their talents on trading and creating foreign exchange possibilities.

Chapter Nineteen

**What you think you must absolutely be doing right at that
particular instant may often not be worthy of doing at all.
It's not just the eyes, open your mind too**

The curse of comfort zones

Currently, all over the world, we are under a curse of hard asset centricity. We are in our comfort zones, our basic conditioning and orientation to stay comfortably trapped in what occupies us every day. We are busy looking at what is just ahead of us and we concentrate on what we face as daily challenges and what is directly visible to our eyes. This is like a bicycle maker who for last 50 years has run a major operation, facing every day in long corridors of offices and the large complex floors full of machines and divisions of factories. The focus is on creating, assembling and manufacturing bicycles and in this noise, chaos and screams, the leadership and top management is basically locked into thinking and worrying about all the hard assets, the buildings, the factory, the floors, the machinery, the inventory and all the rituals that come long. There is no time for anything else. There is no room to visualize ideas. There is just, noise, chaos and screams. They don't realize that they could be creating drones, flying cars, or other types of people-moving vehicles. It is almost impossible because there is simply no time within the day-to-day, noise, chaos and screams that block opportunities from prosperity. Aspects of reinventing, realignments, repositioning are simply not allowed.

Being busy at the day-to-day operation and being caught in the grinding noise of chaos is already considered as great leaps and advancements by the standards of today. Old formatted systems with old productivity processes for creating profitability often keeps the entire organizational creative energies and innovative thinking wrapped in the blanket of curse of hard assets centricity. The curse, morphs our vision by over-focusing on what's in front of us, visible and touchable, as long as it's hard and heavy and ignores the invisibles, like ideas, imagination and vision.

If we are to operate as a symphony, we must begin at the beginning with vision and virtually see the notes of profitability and then approach that vision with complete transparency and team involvement. Each team member must fully understand how their job fits into the whole vision and then perform that part with utter precision. Each day is new and the focus is on the future and better visions.

Today there are over a hundred million plants and factories around the globe with massive outdated infrastructures from the past. They have huge amounts of new and old machinery that is being polished and maintaining same systems every single day. The focus is on keeping the machinery in tip top condition. Bright MBAs are running around the organization trying to cut costs to make some sense in productivity performance and profitability while basically going nowhere. The focus is on keeping the day to day operations functioning, with little or no thought on how to become synchronized organization in touch with the future.

As a proof, just ask any major national trade-association in the world about this. Now for the bright new future; let's explore soft power asset management.

Soft Power Asset Management is the future because it is all about cre-ating productivity, performance and profitability by relying on self-dis-covery for self-optimization, and self-deployments. This means that the readily available 'invisible' and 'untouchable' assets like ideas, innovation, dreams and imagination, entrepreneurialism, critical global age think-ing, planning and creating collaborative alliances and most important-ly a healthy global age attitude towards change are all fully optimized. Soft-power-assets-management is more about execution and deploy-ment and not about new funding and investments, as these soft-assets are around us, unused, un-discovered. Soft-power-assets-management is an invisible goldmine of hidden talents and this goldmine just lies dor-mant in some basement of that doomed castle. Time to huddle and sort all this out with open debate.

The future is driven by talented ideas and new global age is driven by soft assets management.

A quick study of the last 100 major global earth-shattering inventions will easily prove that they were mostly based on soft asset management deployments and happened when they took a dramatic turn away from hard-asset mentality. This study is essential in order to appreciate the heavy losses of operations that are continuously stuck in hard-assets mentality.

Now, let's compare this to some current models. For example, when there is a serious need for productivity, everybody goes after creating maximum capacity building, but that energy is focused in the wrong direction. The energy becomes creating machinery or automation driv-en investments which may not turn out to be prudent in the long run. When performance becomes an issue, management believes that driving the workers to maximize hard work may not the right solutions. They believe this endless struggle is going to increase performance, and they fail to look at how it undermines the entire human resource management and productivity issues. When the need for new profitability is high-lighted, immediately some panicky cost-cutting measures are brought in without measuring the damage they cause. And just think, this could all be alleviated by replacing those bad ideas and putting energy into cultivating good talent, creative ideas, credible problem solving, team involvement, futuristic planning and sensible bottom line approaches.

Overall all the current model results in nothing but disasters, while the answers for these disasters are clearly available.

Let's explore what is needed today

Productivity enhancement is the most critical issue on the table, but it requires maximizing mental capacity building of the organizational management and leadership. Top, middle and bottom parts of the entire organization must all work in total synchronization. Let us not forget the symphony creating music. Organizational harmony comes when the complete team understands and is focused on the goal where roles are clearly defined, operations are transparent, and energy is directed toward the defined goal. Our job becomes finding ways to showcase that the teams are mentally and emotionally prepared on how to enlarge the horizons and operations.

Capacity-building is no longer buying additional equipment. Capacity-building becomes finding and creating sophisticated alliances and linking new sources that expand ideas and center on what can be possible in the future. It features building and exploring global options based on almost free technologies and amazing new styles of business models. Productive today is more about new styles of management execution and mobilizing of smart ideas. This means opening our minds and looking at our hard assets and our soft assets in a whole new way of thinking.

Performance once again requires maximizing the mental and emotional endurance necessary for building teams that have deep understanding of the issues on the table so their performance will achieve and match those desired targets. The old system of performance, where the spotlight is directly related to hard work is replaced by smart thinking and making changes to create sharper turnarounds and better results. This is the future! When mental and emotional stamina are centered on creatively generating prosperity, new doors open and solutions become readily available.

Creating profitability does not necessarily means drastic cost-cutting in all direction, but rather seeking out smart collaborative alliances, intelligent optimization and smart deployment of resources based on the global age research processes that result in achieving productivity performance and profitability. Most importantly if teams are trained like the musicians of an orchestra, the performance will be very relaxed and all team members will do his/her part with confident execution and fascinating ease.

The bottom line is to accept that change is needed in many directions and to realize that simultaneously it is essential to equip teams with a whole new way of thinking. Teams need mental stamina and emotional endurance in order to be transformed as the ultimate drivers of the business…a business that is headed towards the future. In the old days you trained teams to protect hard assets and mentality concentrated on the processes and procedures, the rules and regulations, and the chain of command of the business. Today it's about new thinking and new mental powers and emotional balances. Prosperity today and tomorrow will be about teams moving forward with control, transparency, and innovative approaches for reaching new heights.

The world has changed;

1990 demanded computer literacy and highly educated and experienced executives became ineffective overnight. 2000 demanded e-commerce understanding because without these modern businesses of the day will not be able to run. 2020 now demands that we prove and demonstrate expanded mental capacity and emotional capacity in order to understand global age and comprehend how and why businesses are designed. We must realize how and why they have different sets of procedures and how and why the global age models survive. This new synchronization is focused on how to deploy Artificial Intelligence that will do all of the daily routine and repeated work, so that humans are released to expand their own mental and emotional capacity. Exploration of thought, visioning, and diligent advancing will follow and new leaders emerge.

Smart top leaders of today must focus on creating and demonstrating the elasticity of emotional stamina and accept change in order to survive in the global age. They must focus equally on creating and sustaining physical stamina, for confidence and speedy execution.

The power of knowledge is lost

A hundred years ago, it took almost 100 years to acquire applicable worldly knowledge, and basically by the time you became an expert person it was time to die. Today by the time you're 20 you have more than enough worldly knowledge that is ten times better and a thousand times faster than what it was a hundred years ago. We must realize that by 2025 any ten-year-old will have access to all the global knowledge and will have all that information controlled by simple clicks.

The 10-year-old person may not have the necessary wisdom or experience to utilize it, but the acquisition of this knowledge will be effortless and freely accessible to everyone. In this age of abundance of advance knowledge, everything in society will move quickly and Artificial Intelligence becomes the new norm.

In order to survive in this new and fast-paced new environment, management must truly lead and perform with superior entrepreneurial-based emotional and physical stamina. These will be the driving factors that will create the space for advance innovative thinking and decision-making. In order to survive and move toward prosperity, businesses must lead with new worldly knowledge approaches. New successful heights are waiting to be tapped. The new world has no room or value for classroom learning. The world is now looking for common-sense-street-smart entrepreneurial deployments. The Ivy League case studies of the past have no value. The exclusive power of knowledge is simply lost.

Chapter Twenty

Unless you have been declared almost a lost cause,
you are just one of them

Prosperity roads require self-discovery

The most important aspect of traveling the Prosperity Roads is Self-discovery, this is a very simple yet extremely complicated process. The starting point is expanding and developing mental and emotional stamina. We must discover our own hidden talents and optimize them, we must take our known talents and advance them. Most importantly, we must learn to unlearn, we must relearn to deploy them as a perpetual self-learning and make them the pillars of new knowledge and this type of self-discovery results in smart working. In addition, we must not be afraid to dig deep within ourselves to exceptionally powerful and hidden talents blocked by culture and surroundings but now ready for new global age new challenges.

Now smart working is basically how to utilize minimum resources for maximum results and how to achieve that in the shortest amount of time. Achievement is unlimited because we have access to all the knowledge in the world in limitless time. Individuals and teams become self-optimized, and can quickly see the direction of the enterprise while figuring out the fastest way to get to destinations. Smart working leads to self-optimization. Now self-optimization automatically creates value added performance. Once we have a good understanding of our self, we realize that self-discovery leads to smart-working and on to self-optimization. When this is all combined, there is value-added.

Value added is basically creating superior performance. The superior performance becomes the guarantee for increased profitability. This additional profitability creates liberation, basically freedom from the day-to-day noise of struggling and being in old systems and procedures. No longer held in captivity by old procedures, you are free to think, innovate, and create outstanding results. Liberation from the needs of searching for funding and trying to salvage old procedures, lead to the discovery of growth and open or hidden opportunities within the global market. Competition start appearing less threatening.

So, in order to achieve all this, business ownership must prove and demonstrate they are ready for new critical thinking and ready to embrace the global-age thinking based on improving mental, emotional and physical stamina, to face the advancing technologically and artificial intelligence driven future.

There is no way out. Old education and old knowledge may have educational or experimental value, but they have very little or no application in the future enterprise world.

In order to deploy this new style of thinking and execution, one must also embrace new business models and new styles of thinking and execution such as micro-mobilization. Micro-mobilization is the art of miniaturizing the profitability processes and making them mobile across the organization, within a city, and across the nation or around the globe. It must create the simplest way of replicating processes and procedures, using advanced technology to spread them across the organization. However, this is not about a technology-app or a software program that runs through the heart of the company. This is basically very special advance forms of self-discovered and self-optimized processes and procedures distributed across the organization. The notes of self-discovery and maximized performance move through the organization and follow the like the notes of the symphony.

The rise of restless citizenry

The global citizenry is getting very restless mostly because lack of local grassroots prosperity issues. Based on the performances of the last decade and forecasting the next ones, by the time most current economic crisis around the world reach to any sensible end, the world would be a washed with ecological calamities and global warming disasters. Today, is there any authoritative global leadership with result oriented worldwide consensus and national-global action plans, no, not really. Everyone is waiting for the disasters to hit first.

The incompetency era

As we move forward the grassroots prosperity is collapsing,

The young have no options and the old no patience

Truth is the next weapon against incompetence.

We have to relearn how to fight with our new and real skills and not just rely on drawings and doodles of fake skills.

Social media wit and rhetoric is for the dumb and dumber of organizations

Smart thinking and execution is where the real value creation is hidden. In a world where fakery is more paramount over real value creation, the artistry of sound bites and gibberish is now considered elitism. The world is littered with incompetence at the highest offices of the world and cheered by dumb founded brainwashed cheerleaders. Time has come to unlearn this curse and relearn the art of real value creation, real substance and real growth. The world is slowly awakening to hedge-funded smart cities with clusters of debt-towers where dumb societies get swayed by the winds of fakery.

Incompetency is more dangerous than corruption as it provides fertilization to bureaucracies to hatch corruption

Pick up your arms of special skills and mastery of real value creation and march against incompetency.

Relearn to live in the cathedrals of your mind and buy some robots as your private slaves

Unlearn leadership management stuck in a skyscraper

Learn to become a self-discovered wanderer

Mastery of skill is in your own control, always

Rise of life-long-learners

As the new world becomes fully connected, highly integrated, inter-connected and inter-dependent the powers will be divided by non-learner's nation and re-learner's nations. The massive mechanization of national productivity in will keep masses at slavery rates of income. Advanced level, National productivity will be measured by capacity of nation's mental intelligence. Highly-skilled will have job-security, low-skilled will have limited job-security, medium-skilled will be replaced by robots. To avoid being replaced by smart machines, life-long learners will have a distinct advantage. The highly regimented re-learning processes and contents delivered in militarized styles of rigid and repeated drills on transformational trainings to uplift masses in major nationwide sweeps. Start learning why your skills are not going to fit the future and if not open to new learning the future becomes dark

The fall of the bureaucratic mind

Once, bureaucracy was a sign of nobility and competence which held the structure and integrity of the organizations. Now it has become the biggest global liability on issues of grassroots prosperity. As bureaucracies aged over the centuries fermenting towards incompetency and corruption, they have become a direct burden on prosperity. Today the world is in a deep web of corruption openly managing and executing its operations in broad daylight. The current global economy is like living in a foolish-paradise, under tax-heavens, where special interests in a state of nirvana are the law makers while citizenry skirting around hell is the law breaker.

Globalization of commerce was orchestrated under special interest agenda centricity to help the top layer players of the world of commerce while openly stealing from the bottom layers of the populace. American corporate debt is 9 trillion dollars while Public debt is 21 trillion dollars. The price of glittering success of fake economies. The proof of decimated middle-class and unrest of citizenry around the world is now their reward.

The downfall of branded education

Are top-tier education institution losing their focus. A US $500 billion-dollar private lawsuit is in action now. The largest known college admissions scandal in U.S. history has now surfaced, federal prosecutors are charging high profile parents for paying bribes ranging from $250 thousands to five million dollars to secure spots for their children at elite schools, including Georgetown, Stanford and Yale, all by cheating the admissions process. Is this disaster exclusive to USA only, what else is going on behind Ivey walls? Now, what are the going costs for a fake degree form a top name brand university? What happened to their most brutal selection processes? What is the damage to the credibility of its honest graduates?

215

The escapism to Mars

Outside basic scientific and rocket booster technologies, the notion of colonizing planet Mars not only proves our existence on earth as a total failure, but also for being too destructive and not being fit enough to stay on earth but now happily ready to travel in capsules the size of refrigerators for six months and live in harsh oxygen-less deserts is the most stupid sham of the day.

The rise of dark-data hunters

The rise of psychotics, sociopaths and dark-data hunters of the deep web. Technology has made Metadata the helium for party balloons of the techie-corpo-elites. Now metadata is monitoring all internal, external, personal and intimate information. Psycho-data management, where marketing is going to entrap individuals, prey on their weaknesses and use Psychic and Genomic information to their tactful advantages. they will prey on weaknesses and manipulate people. this landscape will instill fear and raise bars on the suspicious amongst citizenry, causing paranoia. Without technology and some deep world-class understanding on how technology works, nationalism may be able to protect a country from global data-hunters and the deep web. The future will demand more integrity and truth at the highest offices of the land. In 2005 internet reached one billion users, now there are five billion users and counting, by 2025 at least on the commerce fronts billions will be on virtual-reality to start a new golden age. Advanced study is a prerequisite.

Chapters Twenty-One

**When life itself is a constant risk on being dead or alive,
so what's all this fuss about risk taking!**

Innovative models

Self-discovery & self-optimization

At what point in your life will you come to that crossroad where you
will suddenly realize and accept your extreme uniqueness, yours one of
a kind living existence as a human being in this universe? How will you
go forward, deploy your mind and body and showcase your thoughts,
innovations and other hidden skills? This realization will be a moment
of your enlightenment and this cognition will become a bond with mankind for you to play out your hidden obligations to serve mankind and
move towards progress. This is how mankind advances.

Origin of our own and private 'factory of deep thoughts' is still a big mystery, what's our consciousness, where did it come from and where is it
now headed are all mysteries. While, we find our self as being absolutely
one of a kind body and one of a kind minds, unmatched with any of the

current seven billion on this planet is even a bigger mystery. We are not like a termite on a termite hill of a million, we are very uniquely one of kind amongst billions. If we are not all identical than we must prove our singularity with superior performance, we must voice our talents and claim harmony. All over the world, while progressing forward, mankind has comfortably survived for long periods of harmony and diversity all without conflict. Quick timeline study of last 200 years will show that. Our current and prolonged global conflict charts show how the world has swung in a wrong direction and how leadership has become sub-servient to the doctrine where everyone becomes an unspoken-enemy. Old systems are deadweights on thinking, today at a time when global age demands weightless thinking discover your own flying spaces and let imagination wonder.

Time to wake-up

It is time to wake up to reality, sustainability and a common-sense ap-proach to living. the world has been overtaken by a deep destructive dog-ma and until we use our minds to figure all this out, it will increasingly become darker. when shinny lit chandeliers only produce darkness and do not shed light, the mind only is capable of finding that light in the darkness.

Discover your light in your mind.

Unless leadership has the boldness to challenge the vison, unless each management participant is bold enough to challenge their own compe-tence and unless each staff is bold enough to demand audits to allow mix and match capabilities with the assigned littles on business cards nothing will happen. This is all about mental development that leads to positive change. This is all about mental development of each section and division of the enterprise; this is all about the brain power of the entire enterprise as a sum total of all the combined skills and perfor-mances of the people. Study the top ten globally powerful and successful organization and you will not only see how well they succeed but also how easily they manage.

The biggest hurdle is the boldness of the leadership; the biggest challenge to openly accept incompetence as an important pre-transformation stage ready to absorb global age skills, and then realize that the biggest quandary is to allow smart intelligence to take over operations and create room for smart minds to explore additional new frontiers.

This is a simple process but only for smart and open minds dreamers

There are also new corporate styles such as the flat-mobile-hierarchies. Flat and mobile hierarchies are basically teams with deployment strategies designed to achieve maximum impact across the organization. Once again these are not the standard software packages or personal participation as the standard procedures. This is all about mental powers and emotional understanding of the desired targets and new capabilities deploying them in a synchronized fashion so that everything comes together to fit the psyche of global markets. This movement is essential for top corporate management of the mother organization because the symphonic movement of the team moves seamlessly along the roads to prosperity.

The new expansion models of today are based on micro power nations, small countries that are very talented and have the resources and attitudes needed to get organized and participate in global trade. Unlike the superpower nations, who seem more interested in seeking and destroying other nations' economies. Micro-Power-Nations are more self-centered and are concentrating on creating their own identity. Their own exportability, pride and passion are focused within. With some 100 nations in the race for prosperity, it's getting very exciting.

Now to thrive in all these new skill sets adopt the operational style of 'constantly expanding the base'. This execution requires sophisticated training and understanding on how the small, medium or big business should grow. Growth becomes the center of attention and ways are found in order to constantly penetrate new markets in multiple directions with small or big increments. The heart of the business must be always in expansion mode. Once management is fully trained and prepared and ready for increased prosperity, they are ready to understand mobilization which is how to turn their operations into large-scale deployments with little or no added cost. Extra-ordinary saving and large-scale efficiencies become reality.

Furthermore, to manage new styles of operation, adopt the operational style of 'constant-online-presence' This calls for totally new skills in order to understand the new online presence. It is not about a new website or procedures for on line sales. It involves in-depth understanding of how global expansion; image positioning and marketing exposure works and then deployed on a constant basis. Global positioning must be alive and with constant online presence creating constant advancing of the organization's message. Places all over the world are waiting for you if you have the right message, the right way of delivery and a promise so the art is to keep the organization alive and in constant advancing mode to lead the way. This is not simple IT, this type of thinking requires management to come to full grasp with this new thinking, execution, deployment and mobilization styles in order to achieve such mega results with very little costs.

All required components are already and sitting idle within the organizations, but this is a new skills game

The reason such drastic measures are so essential is because by 2025, some 50% of big businesses of the world will drown in new technologies; some 50% of businesses will be overtaken by brand new business models. Some 50% of businesses will be lost because of bad succession planning and some 50% of businesses will fade into black holes because of outdated policies of survival.

At the same time by 2025 some 100 million new and amazing big and small enterprises will emerge. Some 100 million new entrepreneurs will lead and some 100 million new ideas will become the new norm. It is important to remember that America became a one of a kind, super successful dynamic nation by having just 10,000 – 20,000 entrepreneurs who provided and protected the supremacy of America for over a century. Today, India and China alone are adding one billion new entrepreneurs who are currently growing wings and will start flying across Asia and the world in the coming years. This tells us that only those organizations who have the intellectual capacity, mental and emotional endurance, the stamina to understand new thinking, and the understanding of how entrepreneurialism expands will survive.

These exciting new organizations will prosper. With some 100 million midsize businesses around the world, the future for those businesses stuck in hard-asset-centricity-based-future, the future is very dark.

Where are you standing today?

Today it is very important that the big or small corporate leadership is fully aware of where their intellectual capacities stand. What is the level of soft-power-asset capital and their mental and emotional stamina in contrast to all the external factors they face, and all the hard assets they own? It is also essential for them to know where they have parked their empire on the global age, borderless and timeless maps with some understanding of how they will travel on prosperity roads.

All great and once super-successful business knowledge eventually reaches its limits and every decade a new major tsunami of new knowledge arrives to shake down the performance of the organizational world. Such junctions, alters everything and drowns old thinking with extreme brutality. Most leaders and organizations of today are not ready for this brutality.

It is very important to accept the Fact that new competencies are usually created over the layers of old matured and seasoned in-competencies of the past. The base, however, remains the same. Like an ever-growing garden it is a normal process of blooming in different times. Time passes and this process of advancement accelerates further. Denials will keep the personal growth frozen. Refusal to change will destroy enterprises

We must search new revolutionary and advance competencies: the power to use these competencies is already inside us and just need a bit of fine-tuning so they emerge as natural talents. In recent history, filing cabinets were replaced by mainframes. Those mega organizations with billions of file folders, in millions of filing cabinets, parked on massive fortified floors were transformed overnight into one small air-conditioned room of mainframes computers. The art of file management expertise evaporated in new sunshine. We recently witnessed how desktop culture has moved into mobile devices and completely eliminating the old 9-5 office formats and procedures, currently impacting billions office workers around the world.

Prosperity calls for change

What are the next revolutions? What level of smart skills, what types of new intelligence, what speed of smart execution with new technologies, what smart business models with artificial intelligence and what blue prints of regional or global mobilization blueprints are needed for today's prosperity. Today, the biggest challenge is how to take an existing working business model and find passages toward the potential audience of five billion online, connected worldwide customer market bases. Now for those who have mastered the art of 'constant -online-presence'-'and 'constantly-growing-mode', they require mental-emotional capacity as a critical ingredient to such advance global age style operations.

This requires multi-dimensional thinking and execution

Quadrability formation shows us how to think in four dimensions and how to synchronize and execute in four dimensions all working together to achieve four times the productivity, performance and profitability

This level of achievement in performance brings you closer to being the orchestra that produces the finest quality music as an art and as a 'state of being'. This is not where 300 people on the stage are fighting and arguing about their instruments and hitting unplanned notes. It is not about musicians fighting for the conductor's baton or one player trying to play their notes louder than others. The difference between a professional orchestra performing the perfect music that flows seamlessly through the air from the stage and the other ones is that the other performers do not knowing which instrument to play or which notes to hit. They may not even have the right score of music notes. The differences are buried in skills, mutually rewarding goals commonly shared vision. The problems must be unearthed, an enterprise is after a symphony and once all micro-details are practiced and mastered, the rest becomes easy to work.

Any great orchestra producing amazing music as a state of being is really not grinding or manufacturing music; it is simply synchronizing all the various and delicate musical instruments in synchronicity. It is planning each part of the master score and acceptance by each and every member for their part of that score. It demands levels of mastery so that the performance is delivered with full understanding of the final product and the quality of that desired target. Imagine an enterprise, where every member has a most critical role on time to play in order to deliver superior performance. Such transformations are possible with deep immersions and can be implemented within a few weeks to few months.

Senior leaderships need massive preparation. For creating global age comprehension with an edge, it must uncover the hidden talents across the organization. Most of the great or hidden ideas of innovation are just lying around collecting dust. The overly busy nature of operations shuts doors and does not allow innovative thinking to drift through those empty spaces. The majority of existing business models do not have avenues for those innovative ideas to emerge. The most common-sense ideas remain undiscovered because the enterprise is so busy pushing what made them successful in the old days. This style of thinking will not work today.

In order to successfully operate in the digital age, leadership must ignite a deep and silent progress and hunt for new strategies laced with digital solutions. This calls for an appreciation of almost free technologies, understanding of new methods and applications that can open brand new markets, and make the current operation highly agile and profitable. This stage is all about deep and silent progress. This is not about large IT departments but more about nurturing technical and global age thinking.

Leadership for the export age must showcase its global reach and prove that it has the special skill sets needed to open international markets. They must deliver the promise and create sustainable profitability, with style, global age branding and positioning powers. This is not about slogan, logos, and endless advertising campaigns; this all about deep knowledge of image supremacy creation of excellence and innovative thinking, surrounded by world-class Intellectual Property assets. This is all about very superior level performance. It is about delivery with perfection all of the time. Most importantly, it is about the discovery of new global market based wants and needs, and it is about determining new ideas, products, and services that can add value for future development. The roads to prosperity are never straight; they turn and twist, change direction and frequently take unknown routes.

Why are all of the above processes so important?

They showcase and prove that new brain power and new execution and new deployments are less and less about IQ intelligent quotient dependent and more and more about EQ entrepreneurial quotient driven businesses strategy and execution.

The entrepreneurial wisdom is the backbone of the future of the business. Why?

100 years ago, entrepreneurs were considered very strange people and were often jailed.

50 years ago, they were commonly blacklisted as out of box thinkers missing real world realities.

20 years ago, they were automatically given bad credit scores for being adventurous in business

10 years ago, they suddenly become the darlings of the new global political language

Today, all over the world, they are at the top of the list on economic agendas. They have brought new wind, new wisdom and a new dawn to the old dying economies. These new thinkers are now considered as sav-iors; there are worldwide movements with entrepreneurial programs in over 100 countries with all kind of competitive races and awards. These special programs are designed to regenerate entrepreneurialism create new paths for prosperity. This is a great time and an era for nouveau entrepreneurialism and a great opportunity to build national and global enterprises.

Currently micro-power-nations provide extra ordinary new and varied op-portunities for entrepreneurs of the world. This is how they are going to grow.

Fact, entrepreneurialism is in reality chaos in slow motion; The develop-ing and rising economies of the worlds are always in some chaos. They provide the natural blends that will lead to new prosperity and open global markets.

Fact, entrepreneurialism of the new world needs new blood; the world now has the largest majority of youth who bring new skills and increased education. They are technology savvy and equipped with smart phones that give them all the knowledge known to the world. They hold the online knowledge like a degree holder, communicating with incredible speed with understanding how technology opens unlimited global ac-cess. They are ready to spread their wings with this endless supply of new energy, and they are ready to dive into their own economic growth and national causes.

Fact, entrepreneurial ventures badly need early survivability to grow; micro-power-nations are the least expensive countries which provide longer runways to take off for start-up enterprises. All these provide ex-cellent long-term fertile grounds for new ventures. They have nothing to lose and everything to gain.

Basically, the message to entrepreneurial societies of the emerging world, that everything is available. The super success story is waiting for you. There are hundreds of millions of new potential entrepreneurs; there are unlimited free technologies and other resources and the majority of those are freely available. There are five billion potential customers and micro-markets open and when you put together the jigsaw of implementation, the most serious missing piece in the puzzle that becomes clearly visible is the distinct piece of showing lack of key competencies.

Once the issues of creating the superior levels of key competencies needed to match the global edge demands are conquered, vibrant and dynamic economies will change the face of the nation. It can be done country by country or with multiple nations. A new and happier world would emerge on fast track basis.

Back to difficult questions?

A typical good size micro-power-nation can easily export a billion-dollar every day. They don't because they have never accepted this possibility and the acceptance of such ideas would mean that they would have to literally throw their entire current business models and practices out of the window. However, if they wished, they can become business savvy nations by changing and brining massive deployment and new relearning programs into reality and achieve overnight transformation and success. This is all about mind, execution and deployment and not about bureaucracy and more funding. In order to achieve this, it requires leadership to stand up and grasp the knowledge, skills, and attitudes demanded for understanding the new global age requirements. This is about adopting large scale transformation. New global age leadership is about accepting change and leading bravely with openness, inclusion, and creatively.

Discussions at this stage calls for Cabinet Level Meetings to lay out working blueprints and national prosperity and creating international bounce agendas.

Fact, on business education universities have failed and five years of class-rooms may place you ten years behind. Today the knowledge gain is readily available within seconds with a click. The case studies are outdated or do not apply at all in today's world. The old models were good for their time, like 'age of scarcity' where every little new idea was an automatic success. Today we are in the 'age of abundance' where for every smart idea there are 10,000 betters, faster and less expensive ones. The survival in the age of abundance requires special skills tempered for the global age and leadership must demonstrate physical and emotional stamina do understand change and be able to go on this new journey where miniaturization of operations demands very broadened and special mental and emotional capacities. The world is now small and as it passes through the eye of the needle businesses can become lost or they can come out on the other side with as superior performance enterprises with profitability.

The concept is easy; the application is extremely difficult

If we don't understand the hidden powers of soft power asset management, the new world appears as a very dark place. Without an understanding of the deployment of mental powers and realignment of corporate visions and nurturing imagination businesses will be lost, and the new confidence needed to cope will never flourish. Self-discovery is essential so that it can lead to self-optimization. Self-discovery of our own genius can be effortless when you apply the right tools. This is what it's all about; it's our own genius that is awakened and put to work. It is like a giant, with new unstoppable force that creates superior performance. It's the performance that creates profitability, which in return creates the liberation. It's the liberation that creates on-going success. This is how you create and fuel enterprises that makes the stuff of legends.

We must demand proof of new competencies at each and every step of the way; this discovery leads to sharper decision-making and creates superior performances, just like the orchestra creating the music seeks perfection in synchronization and values superior performance.

If you asked 100 leaders of organizations of today, they would all say that they need funding to get all this done. They need funding to develop new products; they need funding to create new innovations; they need funding to open new global markets; they need funding to train new staff; they need funding to buy new technologies.

But in reality, there is no need of funding at all. Call it a big habit, an excuse, or just the way business is run. But when you deploy software asset management and use imagination and vision such issues become available as free tools. When we become technology minded, it's all free. We can create excellence-centric teams. We become more superior in our performance. You just need to create and manage human-talent and transform them into champions. It's all free and it's all about understanding the hidden potentials and talents that resides within us, within our management, within our workers and within our entire organization. Why waste these free untapped, undiscovered, and underutilized and totally abandoned resources? It is extremely easy and at the same time extremely difficult because it is all about changing ourselves and our final approaches to leadership.

To summarize the philosophy; ad hoc and accidental training basically fails, people do not learn in a few days, or few months in a classroom or by taking a course here and there. The changes needed for extreme prosperity require a continuous, long-term approach to creating change. This change requires us to see how almost 100% of entire organization can be transformed in simultaneous synchronization in order to achieve mass transformation on a fast track basis. This is not about training, but rather about decision making in real time on the challenges leaders and teams need in order to function in an environment that focuses on the essentials needed for global market approaches.

This is not some online learning course; this is battlefield of learning in tactical combative formation, where the organization's real wars are fought, conflicts are confronted, and struggles are authentic. Self-discovery of every individual identifies the never-ending talents each team member brings to the business and how those talents can be utilized as the organization moves down the prosperity roads.

It is time for leadership to pick up that baton of leadership, form functioning teams, and conduct the steady hum of synchronized success.

The bottom-line requirement in order to enter into global age performance is to first prepare your mind; first prepare your body; first prepare your heart; first prepare yourself; first prepare your teams, and first prepare your organization. Now you're ready to play in the global age. Discover the sound of your organization's productivity performance and profitability and then sit back, relax and enjoy the profitability.

It's good to be fore-sighted but also very good to be hind-sighted

When you are fore-sighted you can see a huge truck headed your way; when you are hind-sighted you can still note the license plate after the truck has gone over you. Simple point, both are essential; one is to see what's ahead and the other is to understand the kind of trail it leaves. Without such deep observations a lot will get missed, coming and going.

The serious mismatches

Here are key problems commonly found around the world and in both private and public organizations.

Mismatch of job-titles: Most people seriously lack the skills to match their titles. We must solve deeply rooted issues

Mismatch of age: last century and pre-AI thinking is still in silos; Smart thinking is ageless and recreating new culture

Mismatch of culture. Localized thinking is a curse. Create your own global age thinking reach out to the world

Mismatch of procedures. Hard work centricity and old procedures inhibit progress; liberate and replace with technology,

Mismatch of leadership. Accidental lip service leaders must be replaced by new entrepreneurial leadership

The survival kits

Leadership must be active, open, on the front and always active and present. Must be an invincible force

Management must be audited on their business card title to determine what else they possess as real hidden skills. Meritocracy must be followed

Teams and staff, prebriefed, briefed and debriefed and start all over, goal clarification creating one mindshare

Enterprise wide synchronization of objectives to make all small parts combine as a unified force

Outside Battlefields

Vision; well audited crystal-clear objective with no room for illusionary ideas and confusion

Value creation; business model based on integrity to create and serve uniqueness with extreme quality

Image supremacy; professional and authoritative understanding and casual logo-slogan liabilities

Teams; highly compensated, action and reward driven assembly with diversity and gender equality

Driving 2020 and beyond

If you think you absolutely hate your daily grind, and you think you can do much better, then just prove it with your imagination, create that hidden crave for new solutions, dive into the unknown challenges and create something new but solid with quality, design and make it architecturally balanced so it will be strong enough for the national or global purpose.

If you do not understand these hidden powers within your own mind, do not expect any miracles. If you cannot imagine or create the crave, just hum along and keep walking in your designated straight line. Even in your habitat, in your own culture, all under your own skin, this century is still not bad. There is no need to feel bad. This advancement game is not for everyone.

Do not view imagination as 'anger', it is not, imagination is positive, it is vivid, it can come to life and it can achieve immense possibilities. creating and discovering the unknown are inspirational and rare moments that will enlighten a possible solution. an entire scenario instantly playing in your mind as a flash of events which becomes crystal clear and allows the notion of possibilities. it only requires conscious acceptance of this concept, pausing to positioning your thoughts, placing them in order and execute them. as you slowly recognize your own hidden talents to fit into this new journey. whenever you find yourself stuck in entrapments of the day, that is where you will find new bridges to better solutions, better tomorrows and a better self.

Laws of Global-Age-Universality:

Anything online activated anywhere in the world will impact someone somewhere or everyone everywhere.

Ecommerce is now an unimaginable monster size marketplace for every business and person on this planet. Almost free mega platforms, with instant access and global reach; never in the history was such power so freely available to so many people around the clock. What does this mean to every new idea? How are you calibrating for these realities to your own challenges? How fast are you exploring unlimited new markets? How will you turn your lost – opportunities into powerhouse profit centers?

Laws of Global-Age-Image Dilemma:

Every business has a name identity, but NOT all name identities are workable on the new global stage.

The main reasons are that they are too long, too short, difficult to translate and pronounce; have odd connotations, meanings or perception issues. Bad names hurt organizations very quietly and bleed the profits slowly. Good names on the other hand are very unique, distinct, powerful, iconic and globally recognized and respected. Only less than 1% very lucky business names fall in this category, but why?

Laws of Global-Age-Presence:

The concept of "location, location, location" is dead, now it's all about "presence, presence, presence"

Either you are easily accessible around the world or lost in the massive metadata. The new requirements are for the smart players to create overnight successes and by pass century old brands housed in massive old land mark buildings in expensive districts. Advanced global age games being played in the open while the big and old global marketing and branding agencies are simply dying.

World at crossroads:

One way leading towards dark fog and other to bright sunshine and clarity?

The obvious path is not an easy choice as it seems more people are determined to chase the dark fog, but why? The road to clarity is wide open. Innovative excellence is the measurement, extreme value creation is the achieving and achieving iconic global image supremacy is the new standard. The integrity and honest profitability are the ultimate rewards.

Fear not the times, rather the illiteracy unable to read the times.

Fear not the change rather the refusal to change.

Fear not the new global age rather the dark age of slow execution.

Fear not the losing of your job rather clinging to a dying notion.

Fear not the technology rather the speed of transformation.

Fear not the diversity rather fragmented social structures and inequality.

Fear not the lack of prosperity rather poor quality and incompetency.

Fear not the others rather lack of your own self-discovery

The world of conflicts cannot be saved by the last words of the dying soldiers on the battlefields but by discovering the real truth about the agenda centric punditry chasing fake wars. Go out and create global dialogue based on grassroots prosperity, diversity and tolerance based on smart and honest thinking and peaceful living based on human dignity. Engage in open dialogue, engage yourself and engage your surrounding world. Honest dialogue and bold debates will quadruple your performance and open new grassroots prosperity around you.

The starting point is your own quality and speed of self-discovery; the sooner you discover yourself the better. The faster you deploy the easier the process, the higher you reach in your debates and discussions the more exciting the journeys. An amazing future awaits but for the well-prepared ones. Without self-discovery your future may appear dark; without creating calibrated mental journeys to visualize your enterprise in expansion mode the superior corporate performance will remain dormant, without understanding the needs of local grassroots prosperity and its turnaround applications your surroundings may stay trapped in perpetual struggles and finally, without debating high level ideas on the right stages the national mobilization of entrepreneurialism of your nation may stay strangled in unstable economic chaos. Are you an alpha dreamer? Join us

Are you an alpha dreamer?

Join us for high quality major live streaming and podcast events; share your cutting ideas, participate as experts, coaches, moderators, facilitators, corporate or political leaders, national or global entrepreneurs, all ages, genders and reflect on grassroots prosperity and sustainable survivability topics, new business models, stories or strategies.

Lifelong Learning – Perpetual Cycles of Prosperity - Resources

Every other page, amongst these chapters of ideas and suggestions, challenges you to prove and demonstrate your own skills with superior performances. In order to make such analysis happen in a very positive, dynamic and engaging processes there are few very powerful transitional options. For example, world-class engaging and tactical workshops, boardroom level round table discussions, and keynotes or seminars for the entire organization. Large scale national mobilization and deployment programs can be tabled at senior level gatherings or Cabinet Level meetings. All such activities are custom designed to create a powerful impact on an individual, a small or large enterprise or selected regions of a nation. All of our work is guaranteed to be of the highest quality performance with a high return on investment. Our teams are ready to receive your queries and will respond with customized proposals with layout details, value offerings along with our credentials. www.expothon.com

www.alphadreamers.com

speakers@alphadreamers.com

END

INDEX

Acknowledgements

The author and publisher sincerely acknowledge the notable efforts
and special care provided by the following members
of the core production team

Susan Shoemaker

Russ Shoemaker

Linda Shaffer Vanaria

Shelly Frank

Katarina Akman

Alvaro Garrido

Jason Liao

Zurk Ahsan

Author

Naseem Javed

Naseem is a corporate philosopher,
world-class speaker, author and Chairman of Expothon Worldwide;
Naseem, a Canadian, creator of Expothon Strategy
now getting global attention, on how to create 'supremacy of
innovative excellence and business leadership performance' via
high speed 'mass market penetration strategy implementation modules'
and 24x7x365 deployments.

Expothon Worldwide is a Canadian organization
that has developed the Expothon Strategy Global Program.
A think tank on image supremacy of innovative excellence
& entrepreneurial leadership. A decade in the making,
this program is equipped with 100 plus global experts
on innovative excellence, who are ready to transform
up to 100-1000-10,000 enterprises in a region to become
global-age savvy in Tactical and Combative Battlefield Formation
training modules delivered in simultaneous synchronization
as 24x7x365 basis with 100% satisfaction guarantee,
all these programs are integrated in order
to achieve global-age skills.
Videos, details and credential
www.expothon.com

Notes

www.ingramcontent.com/pod-product-compliance
Lightning Source LLC
Chambersburg PA
CBHW031808190326
41518CB00006B/240